An Ugly Little Secret

An Ugly Little Secret

ANTI-CATHOLICISM IN NORTH AMERICA

ANDREW M. GREELEY

SHEED ANDREWS AND McMEEL, INC.
Subsidiary of Universal Press Syndicate
Kansas City

Library of Congress Cataloging in Publication Data

Greeley, Andrew M   1928-
    An ugly little secret.

    Includes bibliographical references.
    1. Anti-Catholicism—United States. 2. Catholics in the United States. 3. Nativism. I. Title.
BX1770.G74   301.45′28′2073   77-13421
ISBN 0-8362-0725-4

Contents

CHAPTER 1

Some of My Best Friends
Are Catholic

I propose in this brief work to discuss the last remaining unexposed prejudice in American life, anti-Catholic nativism. This prejudice is not as harmful to individuals as either anti-Semitism or racism; it nonetheless persists, and a free and democratic society cannot permit the persistence of any prejudice against a substantial segment of its population merely on the grounds that it is, after all, not as bad as some other prejudices. Furthermore, while anti-Catholicism is not as pernicious as racism or anti-Semitism, it is more insidious precisely because it is not acknowledged, not recognized, not explicitly and self-consciously rejected. Good American liberals who would not dream of using sexist language or racist slurs or anti-Semitic jokes have no problem at all about using anti-Catholic language, ethnic slurs, or Polish jokes. They are not hypocrites or fakers or self-conscious anti-Catholics; they are simply unaware of the nativist strains that run through their personalities and the nativist bias in the way they look at the world and describe it.

1

It is very difficult to speak or write on this subject, because anti-Catholicism is a subject most people, Catholics and non-Catholics alike, would prefer not to think about. Those who will listen carefully, sympathetically, and often guiltily to descriptions of racist, sexist, or anti-Semitic bigotry become vigorously and sometimes, it seems to me, irrationally resistant when one recounts evidence of similar nativist bigotry directed at Catholics. A newspaper reporter for a national journal once interviewed me on the subject and asked me for examples of anti-Catholicism. When I began to cite evidence, the reporter dropped her journalistic approach and became an advocate, vigorously arguing with me every inch of the way. She would not have argued, I am sure, against exactly the same evidence advanced by a black, a Jew, or a woman. Some bigotries are fashionable to acknowledge and to expiate; others must be strenuously denied. A psychologist might well see in such a denial the evidence of that bigotry which is most vehemently decried.

Oddly enough, anti-Catholic nativism persists not so much among ordinary Americans as among the nation's intellectual and cultural elites. Within this segment of the population it has become a serious problem precisely because of the increasing number of younger "ethnic" intellectuals who find themselves barred from access to the elites unless and until they repudiate their ethnic Catholic backgrounds. For American society in the years ahead the problem of nativism will be articulated not by the restless ethnic masses (who are, by and large, doing very well in American society) but by the new

2

ethnic intelligentsia that is growing increasingly furious at the discrimination it is encountering. It is the potential for conflict in the confrontation between the ethnic elites and those that dominate the intellectual and cultural life of the country (in the case of New York City, this potential is particularly strong) that has led me to write this position paper.

I know that there is no way I can make all the necessary qualifications, the refinements and nuances that will persuade many readers that I am not paranoid. I can only say that even though I may sound paranoid, the reader should be intellectually honest enough to consider the possibility that I may be right and to recognize that, if I am, the problem I am discussing is a very serious one indeed and ought to be taken seriously. Do not, gentle reader, dismiss me without first pondering the possibility that I may be on to something very important.

I grew up in a liberal Catholic environment; I did not have the "strict" Catholic education that New York media types are wont to believe produces a narrow, rigid, conservative Catholic personality. In the middle western liberal Catholicism of the 1950s, it was taken for granted that nativism was not a serious problem. The election of John Kennedy in 1960 seemed to confirm this assumption (though even then I wondered about the evidence that was collected by my colleagues at the University of Michigan showing that Kennedy's religion had cost him over a million and a half votes). When I left the liberal Catholic subculture to enter, at least with one foot, the elite academic environment of the University of Chicago,

I assumed that the nation's cultural arbiters had long since given up nativism; and when some of my more conservative Catholic friends asked me whether there were any "attacks on the Church" at the University of Chicago, I vigorously ridiculed the possibility. In the decade and a half since, as I have wandered throughout the groves of the academy and the cultural elite, I have been slowly persuaded that I was naive in the early 1960s. Anti-Catholicism, often sophisticated but also often astonishingly blatant, does indeed persist; if anything, it may be even more vigorous now than it was twenty years ago. I would ask the reader who thinks I am paranoid to at least accept proof of my assertion that if I am paranoid, I became so slowly, reluctantly, and against my own proclivities and inclinations. I wish also to be clear that I am making no charges in this volume about self-conscious and explicit nativism. I do not propose to judge anyone's conscience. More than that, I am inclined to believe that very few people realize that they are nativists (though, of course, few people recognize they are sexists or anti-Semites or racists either). The prejudice I detail in this volume manifests itself in inattention, ignorance, and residual bias.

Ultimately it does not matter whether these three behaviors are conscious or unconscious. I do not intend to argue that there are deliberate and self-conscious anti-Catholic bigots. Rather my case is that the persistence of inattention, ignorance, and residual bias in about one-fourth of the population constitutes a serious and, indeed, intolerable problem for a free society.

INATTENTION

There is now a substantial body of evidence that leaves little doubt that eastern and southern European Catholic "ethnics" are seriously underrepresented in various high prestige sectors of American life. The research my colleagues and I at the National Opinion Research Center have done on ethnic achievement (using a composite national sample of eighteen thousand respondents) shows that Polish and Italian college graduates are systematically underrepresented in high prestige occupations. Despite their educational achievements and despite their economic success, college graduates from these two groups simply do not get jobs as good as those offered to British-American and Jewish college graduates. Indeed, the underrepresentation for the two groups is three-quarters of that experienced by Hispanics and half of that experienced by blacks. The situation, then, of the Poles and the Italians is not as bad as that of black and Hispanic college graduates, but it is still pretty bad.[1]

Research done by the Institute of Urban Life at Chicago's Loyola University shows that there are virtually no Polish or Italian trustees on the boards of directors of major Chicago corporations. Such corporations have been adding blacks in limited numbers, but apparently they feel under no compulsion to improve the representation of Poles and Italians.

Research conducted by the Italian-American Faculty Association at The City University of New York shows that while 25 percent of the student body at City

5

University is Italian, only 5 percent of the faculty is Italian—and this despite the availability of a large pool of Italians with Ph.D. training in the New York area. The Italian faculty members are less likely to have tenure and more likely to be appointed as instructors than the typical City University faculty member. Furthermore, in the recent cutback in appointments at CUNY brought on by a financial crisis, the Italians were the first to lose their jobs.

In a case now pending before the Federal District Court for the Southern District of New York, the charge has been made that the twenty largest law firms in the city of New York, with a total of 912 partners, have among them only 15 Italian-American members and only 62 who have graduated from Catholic law schools (as opposed to 298 partners from Harvard, 169 from Columbia, 120 from Yale, and 50 from the University of Virginia). It is scarcely credible that in a city with four million Italian-American inhabitants there should not be more than 15 who are capable of working in the country's most important law firms. As Alan Dershowitz, the Harvard University law professor and civil rights expert who is appearing for Lucido (the plaintiff), comments, "Firms like Cravath, Swaine, and Moore [defendants] have a long history of discrimination. They know how to do it; they've done it for generations." (*Lucido* v. *Cravath, Swaine and Moore,* 75 Civ. 6341, Southern Dist., New York.)

A study of the ethnic identification of members of Congress done by Gerson Green and Richard Shea indicates that the non-Irish ethnics, 22 percent of the

6

population, have only 11 percent of the seats in Congress. Again, their situation is better than that of blacks, who are 12 percent of the population and have only 3 percent of the seats; but they are still notably underrepresented in Congress. (And those who are there, incidentally, have liberal rather than conservative voting records.)

While eastern and southern European Catholic ethnics are approximately 12 percent of the American population, they have only 3.2 percent of the federal judgeships. In the seventh circuit, which includes Chicago with its immense eastern and southern European populations, for example, there is not a single Italian or Slavic judge.

These findings, none of which has been challenged by professional critics, merely substantiate the impression one has that in the upper reaches of American society, Catholics, particularly those whose names end in a vowel, simply are not there. They may be on the faculties of the state universities, but they are virtually invisible on the faculties of the great private universities and in the offices of the major private and public social science funding agencies. Catholics, particularly practicing Catholics, simply are not there. Is it a question of they need not apply? Or is it that they do not apply?

In most cases, those responsible for hiring or making appointments will say that they do not apply. One can only observe that such an argument would not be satisfactory if one were explaining, for example, the absence of a black among professional football coaches, a woman in an academic department, or a Jew at a country club.

These findings (with the exception of the NORC data

7

cited above) are sketchy, and some might say that the scholarly quality of at least some of the research could be quibbled with. However, they suggest a systematic underrepresentation of Catholics in elite positions in American society and do so in terms that would cause an immediate outcry (not to mention more plans for heavily funded research) were the underrepresented group brown, black, red, or female. Furthermore, statistically verified underrepresentation—frequently based on research of no higher quality than that cited in the previous paragraphs—is the basis for a host of federal programs, suits, affirmative action programs, and other attempts to correct injustice. If mere underrepresentation is sufficient to cause action in favor of blacks and women, then why not in favor of Catholics? It may well be the case that the history of racism makes the presumption of discrimination tenable against blacks, but there is a similar (though less severe) history of discrimination against Catholics.

I am not prepared to contend in this essay that the research explicitly establishes that the underrepresentation is the result of discrimination; but I must note that underrepresentation of any other group, especially of the magnitude of, let us say, the underrepresentation of Italians at The City University of New York, would be taken as prima facie evidence, virtually impossible to refute, of discrimination. Why is it not taken so for Catholics? When I ask that question, the answer I get from my fellow social scientists is, either in substance or actual words, "Jews were once underrepresented and blacks and women are underrepresented now in the great universities because of discrimination; but if Catholics aren't there it's because their religion prevents them from being good scholars." And that is that.

I argue, however, that the data cited above proves *indirectly* the existence of nativist prejudice and bigotry. It is not so much the underrepresentation itself that establishes bigotry as the *inattention* to it. In a society obsessed (correctly so, it seems to me) with minority rights, inattention to the underrepresentation of a minority is indeed prima facie evidence of bigotry against that minority. I make my charge of discrimination not on the grounds that Catholics are underrepresented but on the grounds that nobody gives a damn about it. The Equal Employment Opportunity Commission has not processed a single case of discrimination against Italians or Poles; the national press has given the research findings on underrepresentation scant notice; the liberal journals have raised no outcry; those who officially and professionally worry about the problems of society have ignored systematic underrepresentation of Catholics. There are no research funds available to study in any detail the dynamics of such underrepresentation. It is officially not a problem. And that, I contend is bigotry.

IGNORANCE

The second factor contributing to the persistence of anti-Catholicism is simply ignorance about the status and condition of American Catholics. Many of those who live in the groves of the upper academy know more about African tribes than they do about the Catholics who may live across the alley in Cambridge or across the river in Queens or out in the Gage Park district of Chicago (where there is not a great university to maintain racial integration as an alternative to resegregation). Let me cite one example of such ignorance here; other chapters will discuss many more.

In 1974 the prestigious journal *Science* published an article that asserted the intellectual inferiority of Catholics.[2] The methodology detailed in the article was of questionable merit, but more to the point, the data used by the author were more than fifteen years old and did not include even a representative work from the substantial body of literature that had appeared in the last fifteen years showing that the underrepresentation of Catholics in academic careers was a thing of the past. In fact, as the literature demonstrates, from the late 1950s on, younger Catholics have been more likely to move into academic careers than white Protestants; indeed, the evidence shows that they are as likely to have published articles and books and to have tenure in major (though not private, elite) universities as white Protestants.[3] The author of the article apparently felt no obligation to cite the literature contrary to his thesis, which merely supported the conventional wisdom about "Catholic anti-intellectualism." Nor did he feel any obligation to discuss the possibility that, since half the Catholics in the country were immigrants or children of immigrants, the underrepresentation that did exist in the 1940s and early 1950s might have been an immigration phenomenon. Nor would the editor of *Science* publish letters pointing out the inadequacies of the author's method or his failure to cite relevant literature on the other side of the issue. To this day the editor has not acknowledged a single letter of protest.[4]

Now, neither Kenneth Hardy, the author of the paper, nor Philip Abelson, editor of *Science*, can be charged with explicit nativist bigotry, but they can be charged with ignorance of the social change that has occurred in American Catholicism in the last ten years. They are also apparently ignorant, indeed pertinaciously ignorant, of the research literature published in reputable journals documenting that change. In the final analysis the distinction between such ignorance and deliberate bigotry is irrelevant. The bigot lies about the object of his bigotry, the ignorant person ignores the truth even when it is evident and on the public record; in both cases that which is false substitutes for that which is true. From the viewpoint of the Almighty, ignorance may be excused (and I shall leave it to him to judge whether Mr. Hardy and Mr. Abelson are the victims of what we used to call "invincible ignorance"). From the viewpoint of its impact on society, pertinacious ignorance is functionally no different from bigotry.

One may also consult an article in the journal *Ethnicity* by Abraham D. Lavender and John M. Forsyth that reports on the frequency with which various minority groups are studied, as reflected by papers published in the leading sociological journals.[5] Indeed the Catholic minority groups appear to be neglected as subjects for study by American sociologists. In the twentieth century the three major sociological journals in the country carried 482 articles about minority groups in America. Of these, four were about Italians, three about Poles, and one about the Irish (giving that group equal rank with Icelandic Americans). The oldest journal, the University of Chicago's *American Journal of Sociology,* has managed to find two articles worth publishing about the Italians, one about the Poles, and nary a one about the Irish.

The editors of the various journals might well contend that it just didn't work out that they got any publishable articles about such groups. Still, I think, the question might be raised about whether the reviewing process is altogether unbiased in these matters. But even if we concede that an article on blacks or on Jews would not have received a more favorable reading than one on the Irish or the Italians simply because of its subject matter, it is still a terrible judgment on the profession that it has been unable to focus any scholarly interest at all on one-fourth of the population of the country.

Either something is wrong with the sociological profession's perspective on American society or something is wrong with the groups involved. Assuming for the sake of the argument that it is the latter, then one must ask what it is that is wrong. Are they uninteresting people? Inferior? Not worth studying?

Or what?

RESIDUAL BIAS

The third manifestation of nativism comes from what I call "residual bias." Many of my Jewish academic colleagues and friends will admit to considerable unease about Poles because they remember the stories they heard from parents and grandparents about the pogroms in the nineteenth century. I can understand such unease, but I think American Poles could be dispensed from responsibility for what happened when they were not even alive. Usually in such conversations I point out to my colleagues that both Jewish and Polish historians have made an overwhelmingly persuasive case for the argument that anti-Semitism was a phenomenon that came into existence in Poland only in the late nineteenth century, and then in great part because of the Russian skill at playing Polish Catholics and Polish Jews off against each other. Until 1850, relationships between Christians and Jews in Poland were the best in Europe—the reason why so many Jews lived in Poland. The Polish monarchy, for a number of reasons (including the Jewish mistresses of some of the kings), was extraordinarily liberal and enlightened, at least by the standards of its day, in its legislation concerning Jews. One does not want to romanticize the pre-1850 relationship between the two groups in Poland; it would be intolerable by contemporary standards, but it was still the best that existed in Europe. Jewish and Catholic Poles served side by side on the various national revolutionary committees that presided over the Polish

13

struggle for freedom throughout the nineteenth century. Normally my colleagues are unaware of the existence of this literature and are quite surprised to learn about it. To their credit most of them immediately search it out. My point here is simply that we are all victims of the residual folk wisdom we have learned from our families and can only transcend it by seriously reexamining it. As an Irish Catholic, I must reexamine the folk wisdom I learned about blacks, about the English, and about the Italians, too. It seems to me, however, that one can also legitimately expect of Jewish Americans that they reexamine the folk wisdom they have absorbed about Poles and Lithuanians. They also might give the Irish dispensation from responsibility for the times they were beaten up in the public school yards in New York City in the 1930s. I do not see how anyone can seriously be expected to forget the past; however, it also seems to me that in a pluralistic society or even in a just society specific individuals cannot be held responsible for what happened in the past. I never beat up a Jewish kid in the schoolyard (probably wouldn't have been able to, but that's beside the point), and it is not just for me to be blamed for it. Nor would it be just for me to hold against an Englishman who happened to be working with me the centuries of oppression worked on the Irish by his countrymen.

It is fashionable, almost *de rigueur* now, to articulate, objectify, and expiate the racist, sexist, and anti-Semitic feelings one might have had in the past; but there is rather little propensity to do the same thing on the subject of

14

anti-Catholic nativism. I charge that until such objectification and articulation of residual biases occur, those biases will continue to serve as a wellspring of nativist bigotry.

To conclude, I think I have established a strong prima facie case for the persistence of nativism. Catholics are underrepresented in the upper levels of the society, an *underrepresentation* that is systematic and well documented. This phenomenon is treated with *inattention* by most Americans. There is systematic *ignorance* about things Catholic and also a systematic refusal to reexamine the *residual biases* of one's own past. The inattention to Catholic underrepresentation is proven, I think, beyond all doubt. The ignorance and the residual bias described in this chapter are merely illustrations. In later chapters I will provide more examples of both. Piling up examples, however, does not prove the case nearly so well as empirical evidence; thus the principal force of my argument comes frcm the segment that asserts the factual reality of underrepresentation and inattention. The sections concerning ignorance and residual bias are meant to be persuasive and confirmatory.

CHAPTER 2

Present and Past

A nti-Catholicism is as American as blueberry pie. Most serious students of American history are willing to admit that the country has been swept by wave after wave of anti-Catholic sentiment, beginning before the Revolutionary War and culminating in the horrendous outburst of bigotry during the Al Smith campaign.

Allan Chase, in *The Legacy of Malthus*, provides some of the best documentation for the anti-Catholic racism of the end of the nineteenth and the beginning of the twentieth century.[1] Thus, Chase notes, Oxford University's Edward A. Freeman, echoing the racism of Herbert Spencer and Joseph A. Gobineau, "was shocked to find," during his tour of the United States in 1881 and 1882, "that the Teutonic and Aryan Anglo-Saxon bloodlines had been corrupted by the Irish, the Negroes and the Jews. The Irish were far the worst offenders." Freeman commented, "In the oldest of the wooden houses where I went to find the New England Puritans, I found the Ould Ireland Papishes-Biddy" (Chase, p. 107). Freeman proposed a very logical solution to the problem: every Irishman would kill a Negro and be hanged for it.

Francis Walker, the president of MIT, in an 1896 article in the *Atlantic Monthly*, observed: "The problems which so sternly confront us today are serious enough without being complicated and aggravated by the addition of some millions of Hungarians, Bohemians, Poles, South Italians, and Russian Jews. . . . To continue to admit immigrants of these inferior races was only to degrade our own native American race" (Chase, p. 109).

Charles Bennett Davenport, one of the founders of the Immigration Restriction League, described the European ethnics as genetically defective, victims of insanity and epilepsy, criminalism, immorality, low IQ scores, graft, nomadism, shiftlessness, pellagra, laziness, feeblemindedness, asthenia, lack of ambition, and general paralysis of the insane (Chase, p. 116).

Madison Grant, in his *The Passing of the Great Race*, written in 1918, spoke of the disastrous effects on the great American race of the importation of Irish and French Canadian Catholics, and even worse, of the Southern Europeans:

> The result of unlimited immigration is showing plainly in the rapid decline in the birth rate of native Americans because the poorer classes of Colonial stock, where they still exist, will not bring children into the world to compete in the labor market with the Slovak, the Italian, the Syrian and the Jew. The native American is too proud to mix socially with them and is gradually withdrawing from the scene abandoning to those aliens the land which he

18

conquered and developed. The man of the old stock is being crowded out of many country districts by these foreigners just as he is being literally driven off the streets of New York City by the swarms of Polish Jews. [Chase, p. 167]

George Horace Lorimer, the editor of the *Saturday Evening Post,* relentlessly pushed the notion that immigration was a threat to the purity of the American race.

The army IQ test administered during the First World War was also cited as evidence that Russian and Polish Jews, Southern Italians and Hungarians were genetically inferior. Dr. Lothrop Stoddard, in his *Revolt Against Civilization: The Menace of the Under-Man,* warned that the continued immigration of such inferior people would destroy American civilization (Chase, p. 259). And Samuel Holmes, of the University of California, in his *Studies in Evolution and Eugenics,* also relied on IQ scores to warn of the dangers of "receiving hordes of Poles, Southern Italians, Greeks, Russians, *especially Russian Jews,* Hungarians, Slovaks, and other southern Europeans—stocks less closely related to us by blood than the other northern Europeans and less readily embued with the spirit of our institutions. . . . *They show a very high percentage of illiteracy* and they furnish the great part of the unskilled labor of our mines, factories, and streets" (italics added by Chase, p. 261).

Harry H. Laughlin, testifying before a congressional committee, demonstrated the inferiority of the Irish and the Italians by showing that 32 percent of the criminally insane in hospitals were Irish and 23 percent were Italian.

19

Most of the rest of the criminally insane were made up of Russians and Austrians (largely Jews), according to Laughlin (Chase, p. 283).

Reading through *The Legacy of Malthus,* one is astonished and amazed at how pervasive was the racism of the early twentieth century. While there were certainly dissidents, a belief in the superiority of the "Teutonic" or "Anglo-Saxon" or "Nordic" race was the received conventional wisdom for most of the members of America's intellectual elite, and, as Chase has no trouble demonstrating, it was this racism which produced the restrictive immigration laws of the 1920s, aimed principally at southern and eastern European Catholics.

There has been little research, however, on anti-Catholic sentiment in American life since 1930. One encounters in both scholarly and journalistic circles the assumption that anti-Catholicism died sometime between the Al Smith campaign and the John Kennedy campaign, when it was shown to have been definitively eliminated from American life. Indeed, the assumption is so powerful that it has achieved almost mythological status; one who expresses doubt about it runs the risk of being viewed as a bit of a freak.

How did this marvelous transformation occur? Why has there been no scholarly research to document it and the dynamics that accomplished it? It seems to have been forgotten that there were definite anti-Catholic reactions to the Kennedy campaign. And where is the recognition of the fact that just two years before the 1960 election, half the Protestants in the country said that they could not vote for a qualified Catholic for the presidency? Bigotry that is this deep-seated simply does not go away because of one election; the assumption that it does is historically naive. Yet social scientists seem not to have found the subject of anti-Catholicism worthy of serious research. If it does not, by definition, exist, then there is, of course, no reason to study it; one can only say that while such powerful faith in the disappearance of an old American problem may be admirable, it hardly qualifies as serious scholarship.

For a number of years I have been monitoring surveys in which questions have been asked that enable one to examine tentatively the possibility that anti-Catholic feeling persists in our society. The evidence indicates that it not only persists but in recent years has been increasing, especially among Jews and blacks. I have repeatedly brought this to the attention of responsible funding agencies and urged that more elaborate and intensive research be done—not necessarily by me. To date nobody has been willing to initiate so much as discussion of the possibility. Anti-Catholicism in the United States has not been studied in the last fifteen years, and the reason is that those who initiate and sponsor social research do not want to investigate it, despite strong a priori reasons for assuming that it persists and some empirical confirmation that the assumption is a valid one. In other words, it is a secret because there are a lot of people who want to keep it secret.

The 1976 presidential campaign offered plenty of

evidence to anyone who was interested that the old stereotypes about the "Catholic hierarchy" are alive and well. I personally do not approve of abortion, but I disapproved of the bishops' seeming involvement in the presidential election on that issue because I thought their strategy was inept and counterproductive. (This feeling seems to have been echoed by a majority of the hierarchy at a pre-election administrative board meeting during which they effectively repudiated the strategy of their own executive committee.) Nevertheless, the outcry from columnists from every part of the political spectrum carried enough anti-Catholic resonances from the past to scare anyone who paid attention to them. James Kilpatrick, Mary McGrory, Jerald terHorst, James Reston, and Clayton Fritchey all denounced the bishops for violating the boundaries of "separation of church and state." Indeed, Ms. McGrory went so far as to accuse the bishops of violating the separation of church and state even by meeting with the presidential candidates. The Religious Coalition for Abortion Rights (made up of Protestant and Jewish groups) charged the bishops with introducing "religious dogma" into the election campaign and thereby violating the boundaries between church and state.

Now one can, in a pluralistic society like our own, disagree strongly with the position the Catholic hierarchy took on abortion. But one must raise the question as to why a group of religious leaders who express an opinion on a moral issue should be accused of violating the separation of church and state. A religious coalition can take a stand in favor of abortion, but that does not violate constitutional principles; when the Catholic hierarchy takes a stand against abortion, it is a violation of constitutional principles. One is forced to conclude that it becomes a violation because the laws of separation of church and state apply only to the Catholic hierarchy or apply to them in a special way. Rabbis can meet with presidential candidates on Israel, and that does not violate church and state boundaries; Protestant ministers can actively campaign for Jimmy Carter (as did James Wall, editor of the *Christian Century,* and a militant defender of the separation doctrine), and that does not violate separation of church and state; various local, national, and international church assemblies can pass scores of resolutions prescribing what ought to be done morally and religiously on almost every facet of American foreign and domestic policy, and no one protests that these worthy churchpersons are illegitimately meddling in church politics. Only the Catholic hierarchy, it seems, acts illegitimately when it raises a religious and moral question about public policy.

How come?

The answer, it is to be feared, is that suspicion and hostility toward the Catholic hierarchy have always been a part of American life and remain a part of it. There can be no other explanation of why responsible and intelligent commentators seem able to apply a double standard for religious leadership without, apparently, giving the matter a second thought.

The persistence of nativist categories also explains

the extraordinary preoccupation of the national media with the abortion issue during the 1976 campaign. All the available evidence indicates that the abortion issue influenced less than 1 percent of the American population (and the pro- and anti-abortion forces actually canceled each other out). All the available evidence indicates that there is little difference between Protestants and Catholics in the range of attitudes toward the legalization of abortion. Most Catholics distinguish between abortion as a personal decision, which they reject for themselves, and abortion as a legal possibility that ought to be available to those with other moral viewpoints. There is also little difference between Protestants and Catholics in their attitudes toward the appropriateness of abortion as the subject of a constitutional amendment. There was simply not a single iota of evidence advanced during the campaign that the abortion issue was affecting Catholic voting behavior in the slightest. And yet, time after time after time, *Newsweek, Time,* and the *New York Times* spoke of abortion as "the Catholic issue" and linked the low level of Catholic enthusiasm for Governor Carter with the abortion question. In its issue after the election, (November 9, 1976) *Time* spoke of the "defection" of the Catholic ethnic because of the abortion issue, noting that Carter's victory had been brought about by white Protestants, who canceled out the Catholic "defection." The magazine cited no evidence that Carter lost Catholic support because of the abortion issue; in fact, he won substantially more Democratic votes than did George McGovern. How a population group can "defect" when

24

the proportion of its vote for the party's candidate has increased over the past election is a mystery that will have to be left to the wise men of *Time,* Incorporated. How a population group (white Protestants), a minority of which voted for the candidate, "saves" an election that is being lost by another group, a majority of whose members voted for the candidate (56 percent of Catholic voters chose Carter), is another mystery *Time,* Incorporated, will have to explain.

Unless, of course, one chooses to see the ghost of a Catholic plot orchestrated by the Catholic hierarchy and carried out by the Catholic masses. Such plots were taken for granted in the past; anyone with familiarity with the historical literature will have no trouble finding parallels between the alleged Catholic "interference" in the 1976 election and the "rum, Romanism, and rebellion" of the 1876 election. The themes are muted now, more sophisticated, less overt than a century ago; but how else can one explain the media-created "Catholic abortion issue" and Catholic "defection" for which there was virtually no evidence at all?

It was also said, without any supporting evidence, that Catholics were skeptical of Governor Carter's Baptist piety and that cultural differences between Catholics and Baptists accounted for much of the Catholic resistance to Carter. Such cultural differences, of course, did not prevent Catholics from voting for Harry Truman or Lyndon Johnson, and none of the pollsters was able to find any disproportionate trace of concern among Catholics about Carter's religion. Indeed, the percentage of Catholics who did express concern about his religion (9 percent) was exactly the same as the national average and half of the percentage for Americans who had graduated from college. How then did the issue of Carter's religion emerge? One is forced to conclude that it is another ghost out of the past in the fashionable garb of the present. The journalists and commentators who are haunted by such ghosts are doubtless unaware that they are using the categories and stereotypes of the nativist past. One would not accuse them of religious bigotry, but one must still ask why they are unaware of the nativist origins of their perspectives. One might also ask whether, finally, it makes any difference whether their anti-Catholic bias is deliberate or not.

Yet there is an adequate if not extensive literature on nativism. John Higham, Edwin A. Moore, and Ray Allen Billington, for example, have dealt with various historical manifestations of nativist prejudice.[2] These authors document the bitter history of anti-Catholic bigotry that goes back to the very beginnings of the republic. "Both the Puritans of Massachusetts Bay and the Anglicans of Virginia, despite their many differences, shared the fear and hatred of Rome.... The settlers themselves had been cradled in an England more bitter against Catholicism than at any other time."[3] Convents were burned, priests were lynched, and laymen were murdered; vicious propaganda tracts were published, Catholic schools were closed by state legislation, Catholic leaders were vilified, Catholic immigrants were caricatured, and Catholic prejudice given official sanction throughout the entire nineteenth century. Catholics were papists, they were foreigners, they were not Anglo-Saxons, they were ignorant, they were racially inferior, they were a threat to the American way of life, they could not be assimilated into American society; they were dirty, they drank too much, fought too much; they were no better than animals and substantially inferior to freed black slaves; they voted the way their priests and political leaders told them to vote, they were conspiring to bring the pope to rule America; their schools were sources of foreign propaganda, their priests raped nuns. You could not be a good Catholic and a good American because of your dual allegiance to the pope as well as the Constitution; you could not be a Catholic and a good scholar because the Catholic mindset was antithetical to objective scholarship (one prominent faculty member at the University of Chicago in the 1960s was heard to argue that he could no more accept a Catholic as a colleague than a card-carrying Communist and for the same reason). Italian immigrants were innately criminal, Polish immigrants innately unstable, Irish immigrants innately corrupt and alcoholic. The Know-Nothings, the American Protective Association, the Patriotic Order of the Sons of America, the Junior Order of United American Mechanics were the most famous, perhaps the most notorious, of scores of anti-Catholic organizations. The Ku Klux Klan in the 1920s was more anti-Catholic in the North than it was antiblack. It controlled a number of state legislatures and exercised strong influence in many others. *The Menace* had a circulation of several hundred thousand, and *The Awful Revelations of Maria Monk* (phony confessions by a former nun) sold hundreds of thousands of copies.

There were two streams of nativism, one anti-Catholic and the other antiforeign. At certain times and with certain groups one element was stronger than the other, though the two intertwined so intricately that it is frequently difficult to sort them out. Surely in the restrictive immigration legislation of the 1920s and in the frantic agitation that led up to such laws, the antiforeign component of nativism took precedence. Greek Orthodox and Polish Jews were no more welcome than Polish or Italian Catholics; the grounds for their exclusion were racial rather than religious. The "ethnic" stereotype of today reflects the antiforeign sentiment of the twentieth century somewhat more than the anti-Catholic sentiment of the nineteenth century. But it matters relatively little to those who were and are the victims of such prejudice.

That Polish, Irish, or Italian Catholics could not be good Americans was widely assumed to be true in the United States at least until the 1920s. And judging by the presidential elections, it was true even into the 1950s. You could not be a good American because of your superstitious religion, because of the constraints of ecclesiastical discipline (a line out of the past that Mr. Justice Powell inserted in a recent Supreme Court decision), because you were dominated by your clergy and your scheming, plotting hierarchy, because you owed allegiance to a foreign prince, because your family life restricted economic achievement (as Gerhard Lenski, an American sociologist, said in the early 1960s), because your peasant cultures and disorganized family life equipped you poorly for American society, because you were congenitally drunken, criminal, or unstable, because you were racially inferior, because you went to bad parochial schools, because you were led by corrupt politicians, because you did not have the ambition or the energy to work hard like other Americans, because the commitment to Catholic faith impeded serious, open-minded, intellectual research, because you worshiped the saints and the Virgin Mary, because you thought what the priests and bishops told you to think, because you had old-fashioned sexual ideas, because your religion was incompatible with modern science. If Catholic superpatriotism emerged as a reaction in the 1950s, it was small wonder.

That anti-Catholicism has been a major theme of American culture is, I think, not questioned by responsible historians. Yet that theme receives relatively little attention in the standard grammar school, high school, and college history books. One is hard put to find in the catalogues of the elite universities any graduate school course offerings or seminars on the subject. Racism, of course, is acknowledged and emphasized (as it should be), but why do we ignore its half brother, nativism? Maybe you can be intellectually honest and acknowledge the one while you ignore the other; I don't see how.

The United States has never really acknowledged the

nativist problem. The restrictive immigration laws of the 1920s have indeed been rejected, but the country has never faced the fact that these laws were based on a vicious racism (in the sense of the "Nordic race" or the "Anglo-Saxon race"), a racism that was supported by many of the "right" people (E. A. Ross, Francis Kellnor, Senator Cabot Lodge, among others), the civic leaders, the "good citizens," who either actively promoted nativism or at least remained silent in the face of it. No one rose to defend the Irish in the nineteenth century or the Italians and the Poles in the twentieth. The University of Chicago "school" of sociology descended on the Polish slums on the northwest side of Chicago with pencils and notebooks to record the instability of a disrupted culture and to argue a mitigated form of nativism. The immigrants were not racially inferior, they were culturally inferior and "socially disorganized." To be culturally inferior was a substantial improvement, of course, on being racially inferior, though many of the Polish immigrants might be excused for feeling angry at being so described by the Chicago sociologists. And in fact, the country's intellectual and cultural leadership has never really repudiated nativism the way it has repudiated racism and anti-Semitism. It has never offered sympathy to the past and present victims of nativism the way it has offered it to the past and present victims of racism; it has never really officially legitimated the right of Poles and Italians and Irish to be Americans the way it has legitimated the right to freedom of Jews and blacks. On the contrary, it is the intellectual, and frequently the biological, descendants of those right-thinking people who applauded the restrictive immigration legislation of the 1920s who today continue to insist upon the stereotype of the white ethnic, blue-collar hard-hat. Moreover, the white ethnics are expected to expiate the racism of the past because they still happen to live in urban neighborhoods and have not been able to flee across suburban boundaries. One can forgive the "ethnics" for thinking there might be some hypocrisy at work in such judgments of them.

Historically, the link between the early twentieth century image of Poles as racially unstable and incompetent and the Polish ethnic joke of today is clear. So, too, is the link between the stereotype of the hard-drinking Irish buffoon of the nineteenth century and the caricature of Daniel Patrick Moynihan served up by the media. So, too, is the link between the image of the corrupt Irish politician of the nineteenth century and the stereotyping of the late Richard Daley's Cook County organization. So, too, is the link between the earlier belief in the innate criminality of the Italian and the image of the Mafioso in *The Untouchables* and *The Godfather* or the extra-legal Italian cops like Baretta and Delvecchio. So, too, is the link between the feared hierarchical plot of the nineteenth century and the hierarchy's violation of the separation of church and state by taking a moral stand on the abortion question. So, too, is the link between the stupid Catholic masses voting the way their religious leaders tell them to vote and Jimmy Carter's "Catholic problem" of the 1976 election.

An outsider, coming to American society from, let us say, another planet, would have no trouble recognizing the structural, functional similarities between the myths of the past and those of the present. *The Nation*'s outraged horror during the last election at the profoundly reactionary "ethnic appeal" of Daniel P. Moynihan recalls similar expressions of dismay over the threat to American freedom of massive numbers of "foreign" voters. The language is almost the same, the images are almost the same, the fears are almost the same. The rhetoric may reflect the changing American styles of expression rather than any substantive change in American mythology. A bigotry that was explicit and out in the open was at least easy to deal with; that which has become unself-conscious and muted is much harder to exorcise.

I am open to persuasion. Maybe the imagery of the 1970s, the 1920s, and the 1890s is only accidentally similar; maybe there is no direct historical or cultural or intellectual linkage. This can only be established, however, when someone bothers to do the basic research that is necessary and someone else bothers to fund such research. Until then, the striking morphological similarities between the images of the past and those of the present must certainly suggest strongly that the old prejudice is alive and well. Again, the evidence is necessarily indirect. One might argue that the absence of concern about the persistence of such imagery indicates that the old prejudices are still with us. Those who are terribly concerned about the stereotyping of some groups in society and ignore the apparent persistence of historically biased stereotypes of others must be found at least indicted by prima facie evidence on the charge of perpetuating bigotry.

A word about the Catholic vote: during the 1976 Carter campaign, there was an implication in much of the discussion of Carter's "Catholic problem" that the very existence of a "Catholic vote" was somehow reprehensible; correspondingly, the possibility that the "Catholic vote" might virtually have vanished from American society was seen as a sign of enlightenment and progress.

Now why a Catholic vote should be any more reprehensible or reactionary than a Jewish vote or a black vote must remain a mystery. The majority of Catholics like the majority of Jews and blacks vote Democratic. There are a number of historical reasons for this—the Republican party was much more likely to be nativist in the North; it had supported Prohibition (which was viewed by immigrants as anti-Catholic legislation) and the nativist immigration legislation of the 1920s. It was the party of business and of the rural areas, and the Democrats were the party of the workers and the urban areas. Jews, Catholics, and, after 1932, blacks found the Democratic party more sympathetic to their interests and more likely to support policies they supported. (Despite the myth, on most social and economic legislation Catholics continue to show "liberal" sympathies.) In congressional elections from 1952 to the present, Catholics have voted on the average at a rate between three-fifths and two-thirds for Democratic congressional candidates. They apparently did so again in 1976. In the

33

presidential elections of the same period, the average Catholic vote for Democratic candidates was around 62 percent—until the McGovern fiasco of 1972, when for the first time, Catholics voted in majority numbers for the Republican presidential candidate. So there was and still is a Catholic vote; it is simply a Democratic political vote, rooted in historical and contemporary political, social, and economic issues and not in specific religious concerns. Carter ended up with 56 percent of the Catholic vote, substantially more than Senator McGovern, somewhat less than Senator Humphrey. Apparently, in the waning days of the campaign, he won the undecided urban Democrats in substantial numbers and failed to win over undecided suburban Catholic voters in any appreciable numbers. These facts about Catholic voting patterns are a matter of public record and have been analyzed, explained, and written about in scores of articles and monographs by political scientists for the last two decades. There ought to be no mystery about them. The attempt to represent the Catholic vote in the 1976 election as a dangerous, reprehensible, scary, exotic, or bizarre phenomenon can be only explained by a sudden attack of ignorance about the fundamentals of American coalition politics.

There is no reason to believe that now or at any time in the past has the Catholic clergy or hierarchy been able to "deliver" the votes of Catholics. Catholics voted for Democratic candidates for reasons that had little to do with their clerical and hierarchical leadership. The myth of votes controlled by the church has never been

34

substantiated by historical or sociological evidence and runs against all the folk wisdom and what little careful study has been done about Catholic political behavior. The hierarchy has rarely in the last fifty years tried to use its political muscle, and when it has done so, it has achieved little success. Indeed, probably the only such success in the whole history of American politics was the alliance between Catholic and Lutheran forces to defeat laws that tried to outlaw parochial schools. The hierarchy has had little political influence—partly by wise choice and partly because of ineptitude and incompetence. The image of Cardinal Spellman sitting in his "powerhouse" on Madison Avenue and influencing the outcome of the New York elections may have been useful for frightening children growing up in that city who no longer believed in the bogyman, but it corresponded to no reality that anyone has ever documented or that any professional Catholic politician ever took seriously.

Doubtless there have been times when bishops have tried by a phone call or a meeting at a wake or a funeral to influence Catholic politicians. Presumably clergymen of other faiths have not refrained from using such encounters to influence politicians. But systematic, persistent attempts to control the political order by Catholic bishops have never been documented. It is extremely unlikely that such incidents could occur with any regularity without documentation emerging.

From the inside of the Catholic community, the thought that bishops call the tune and the laity dance to it in politics or any other matter is ludicrous. The history of endless ethnic competition, conflict, and compromise within the American hierarchy and church, which has been richly documented by Catholic historians, makes the massive, monolithic image of the Catholic church seem absurd. But the internal differentiation among Catholics has been a hard phenomenon for many Americans to comprehend. If pushed, most commentators would probably admit that bishops probably don't deliver very many precincts, but the internal dynamics of the Catholic community seem to have escaped them.

The simple truth is that blue-collar Catholics voted overwhelmingly for Jimmy Carter (62 percent). They will continue to vote Democratic because their political and economic interests and their traditional loyalties induce them to do so. Suburban Catholics are caught in a bind between their traditional loyalties and their upper-middle-class social and economic interests and will increasingly move back and forth in presidential elections; apparently they will continue to vote Democratic in most congressional elections. Such swings in the voting patterns of upper-middle-class Catholics will be very little influenced by the hierarchy, and most of the members of the hierarchy know that.

CHAPTER 3

Ignorance

L et us begin with a number of statements about American Catholics.[1]

1. Catholics tend to be blue-collar workers and lower middle class. Educationally and financially they do not compare with their Protestant counterparts. A Catholic background makes it less likely that a young person will choose an academic career or, should he choose one, do well in it. Those Catholics who do become successful academics will leave the church. Irish Catholics, who have been in the United States longer than other ethnic groups, have achieved a certain amount of modest respectability, but they have not made the most of their opportunities in the New World—perhaps because of their religion, perhaps because of their family structure, perhaps because of their drinking habits.

2. While they have traditionally voted Democratic, Catholic ethnics are conservative. They are more likely to be racist, less likely to support civil liberties, more likely to take a punitive attitude toward the counterculture. They were stronger supporters of the Vietnam

war than other Americans and voted heavily for Wallace in 1968. As many of them moved into the suburbs and became more affluent, they began to drift away from the Democratic party in both affiliation and voting behavior.

3. Most Catholic priests are not happy in their vocations. Those who have left the priesthood are the best and the most talented. The commitment to celibacy makes it impossible for a man to develop capacities for openness, intimacy, and sympathy with human frailty. Most Catholic clergy would marry, given the choice.

4. While Catholics are more likely to be against abortion than Protestants, the opening up of the church in the Second Vatican Council has caused a notable decline in Catholic religious practice. The encyclical letter on birth control, *Humanae Vitae*, however, caused serious moral anguish for large numbers of American Catholics.

5. Catholic support for Catholic schools is declining, mostly because Catholics now realize that in the suburbs where they now live the public schools are better. There is little willingness in the Catholic population to make the financial sacrifices required to keep parochial schools in operation. In any event, there is no evidence that parochial schools make their graduates any more religious than they would have been had they gone to public schools. Parochial school graduates are more likely than public school graduates to have hostile attitudes toward blacks and Jews and are less likely to ˉbe well equipped for success in American society.

It is not an exaggeration, I think, to say that all five

of the above paragraphs seem unexceptionable. They are a fair portrait of what everyone knows to be true about certain aspects of American Catholicism. Why would one waste time, effort, and money to collect social science data to support such obviously true statements?

In fact, every single one of the above propositions is demonstrably false. For each there exists empirical evidence to demonstrate that they are not true, and in fact, in many cases, to demonstrate that the opposite is true. For example, the Irish are the most successful gentile group in the United States both financially and educationally. Support for Catholic schools has not declined in the last ten years, and there is very considerable willingness among Catholics to provide the schools with financial support—and this is as true for Catholics in their twenties as it is for those in the older age cohorts. Catholics did not support Wallace in any appreciable numbers. They have not drifted to the right politically, and they have not left the Democratic party. Catholics are no longer disproportionately blue-collar workers. On the contrary, they are more likely to be members of the middle class than Protestants (taking into account race, region of the country, and urbanism). Most Catholic priests are happy in their work, and only a minority would marry if they were free to do so. Psychological testing does not show them to be deficient in their capacity for intimacy. I could go on.

Ignorance is neither criminal nor sinful in itself, of course, but ignorance about a major segment of the population (about one-quarter) among those who make public policy, articulate basic issues on the social agenda, and seek to inform and interpret public opinion is at best a form of unconscionable negligence. If stereotypes and images of bigotry persist, the reason is that such symbols are very useful in interpreting and organizing experience when one does not have accurate information. Furthermore, if experience is sufficiently well organized by the symbols of bigotry, then one need not bother to gather information. As I suggested in chapter two, the Catholic hierarchy-Catholic vote symbols that were resurrected in order to "clarify" the abortion issue in the 1976 election represented in fact a continuation of the fears and bigotry about the massive, monolithic Catholic population, made up of conspiratorial leaders and ignorant masses, that arose long ago and are as American as blueberry pie.

Similarly, the Catholic racist stereotype symbol is completely immune to exorcism by empirical evidence. It is also useful in organizing and interpreting Catholic behavior. The combination of the racist symbol and the monolith symbol seems to have provided for most commentators and columnists sufficient explanation of the reluctance of Catholics to jump on the Carter bandwagon (*Time* explicitly mentioned race as one of the reasons for the "Catholic defection"). But if you are simply dealing with racists and conspiratorial bishops, you do not have to seek any other explanations. Ignorance under such circumstances becomes intellectually useful. When someone points out that in the North various affirmative action and positive discrimination programs that are limited to cities will almost inevitably discriminate against Catholics, you might be astonished. It had never occurred to you that positive discrimination in favor of blacks might entail discrimination against Catholics. You could then console yourself with the thought that since Italians tend to be racist, such treatment serves them right. If you are then informed that the Italian scores on racist scales are lower than the average for white northerners, you have a very difficult fact to digest. The easiest thing is simply never to inform yourself; it's much simpler when you have never heard the facts in the first place or never been constrained to face them.

I do not intend to be cynical, but in a professional career devoted to examining myths about Catholics and finding that they are not true, I have discovered that empirical evidence is a very weak weapon to use against entrenched ignorance. In the absence of any other explanation for the power of ignorance, I must conclude that some people want to be ignorant because it simplifies their world view and justifies their social policies.

Ethnics are no longer disproportionately blue-collar workers, but the blue-collar ethnic stereotype persists. The Irish are the most economically successful gentile group in American society, yet the stereotype of the shiftless Irish drunkard persists; the Polish college attendance rate has crossed the national average, yet the stereotype of the ignorant Pole persists. Catholics are now more likely to pursue academic careers than Protestants, yet the stereotype of the anti-intellectual Catholic persists. Catholics cheerfully and enthusiastically support their schools, but the stereotype of the school maintained (in Mr. Justice Powell's words) "by the constraint of ecclesiastical discipline" persists. Catholics are more liberal on social issues and less likely to be racist in their attitudes toward blacks than their white northern counterparts, but the stereotype of the conservative and racist Catholic persists.

When I trot out the evidence that demolishes the myths, I rarely get an indication that there has been any change of mind. The evidence is denied or rejected, the methodology questioned. I am especially appalled to encounter such entrenched and what often seems deliberate ignorance among scholars who are supposed to be devoted to a dispassionate, objective search for truth. The same people who are totally dedicated to the elimination of stereotypes about blacks, women, or Jews are not interested in the evidence about Catholics and are unprepared to accept it when offered. I wonder why.

Furthermore, to conduct research on that one-quarter of the American population that is Catholic is virtually impossible in the American academy, particularly if the research requires large-scale funding. Catholics are not an interesting subject for research, or there is nothing worth knowing about them, or it's not the kind of activity for which you can expect to get tenure, or it would be encouraging divisiveness to study them, or it's a violation of the separation of church and state. Again the issue is not so much the fact of ignorance but the easy and casual acceptance of it that reveals the ugly little secret. You may not be a bigot if you think Italians

42

and Poles are still poor, you may not be a bigot if you are uninterested in their poverty, you may not be a bigot even if you don't want to fund research or grant faculty status to people who do fund research on Italians; but it seems to me that you are most surely a bigot if, when you are presented with evidence that illuminates the darkness of your ignorance, you refuse even to acknowledge it.

The problem is reinforced by those to whom elite Americans turn for guidance, interpretation, and explanation concerning things Catholic. Some national publications, most notably, *Time, Newsweek,* and the *New York Times,* have religion editors who are sophisticated and well informed about Catholic matters. When these writers are permitted to have their say, the material that appears is accurate and perceptive. Unfortunately, on political, racial, and social matters, the well-informed religion editors are usually sidetracked in favor of confident and certain but very ill-informed writers. Anyone who knows Catholicism from the inside is appalled when such writers use quick and easy sentences to explain that "the Catholic problem" with Jimmy Carter was abortion and that the urban ethnics' unease about positive discrimination is racist, or to identify the ethnic as a blue-collar hard hat. And then we read that there are massive revolts among the laity, frustration and unhappiness among the clergy, and that political and social activism is the primary concern of young Catholics. All of these themes fit the stereotypes; they dispense one from examining the facts and perpetuate the nativist anti-Catholic myths around which the stereotypes are built.

The fundamental nativist assumption has always been that the Catholic church will be in trouble as soon as enough of its members become sufficiently well educated to see through its foolish superstitions and its arrogant abuses of power. So when various interpreters of the recent crises in American Catholicism assure their readers that this is exactly what's happening, then that is good news, indeed. Both Wilfrid Sheed and Garry Wills have played that role (Sheed in the *New York Times,* Wills in his book *Bare Ruined Choirs*), and they play it with a graceful and elegant literary style. Let us weep for the bare ruined choirs and the lost confidence in the old doctrine, and in the meantime let us turn to Berrigan activism for meaning and purpose in life. So says Mr. Wills, and the unconscious nativist applauds enthusiastically. Similarly, Mr. Michael Novak (*Rise of the Unmeltable Ethnic* [New York: Dell, 1974]) titillates nativist fears of the militant ethnic and talks about an organization that has ethnic millions, most of whom, as Mr. Novak describes them, behave just the way the nativist knew they would.

One vainly points out that Mr. Sheed, Mr. Wills, and Mr. Novak have spent little time in Catholic neighborhoods recently or that they have not attempted any systematic collection of empirical data. One vainly notes that their efforts are primarily autobiographical and that there are other, somewhat younger, scholars who have been grubbing away in systematic research. What these social scientists and historians have been discovering is what the elite reader doesn't want to hear; he much prefers an analysis of Catholics written in the *Village Voice* by Mr. Geoffrey Stokes, who informs him that Archbishop Bernardin, the president of the American hierarchy, is the archbishop of St. Louis. I wonder if such stupidity would be tolerated if the object of it were anyone but Catholics.

The amateur, then, is preferred to the professional, the autobiographer to the scholar, the alienated outsider to the sympathetic insider, the person who rejects the neighborhood to the person who still lives in it, because they say what people want to hear. If that isn't bigotry, I don't know what is.

When I began my academic career I was a naive innocent. I thought people took evidence seriously. My first research enterprise tested the conventional wisdom that Catholics were not choosing academic careers. I believed the conventional wisdom to be true and wanted to explore the dynamics of such antiintellectualism. But our data showed just the opposite—that somewhere between 1950 and 1960 there had been a complete turnaround, and that now young Catholics were going to graduate school in massive numbers. I assumed that such evidence, based on incontrovertibly good sampling methodology, would be readily accepted by the scholarly community. To my astonishment and dismay I could not have been more wrong. Now, a score or more of scholarly monographs and articles later, I find that the stereotype is still unshaken.

It seems to me, therefore, that much of the ignorance

about American Catholics is willful. It derives not merely from unawareness of the facts but from a deliberate refusal to face them, a tenacious clinging to old stereotypes because the pain of giving them up is unacceptable.

If the reader says, "Well, maybe he's right; maybe we don't know much about Catholics; maybe the things we thought we knew were wrong. Maybe we ought to spend more time, money, and energy learning about them, because they are one-quarter of the population, after all"—such a response could not be classed as bigotry, I think. However, if the reader simply dismisses the research evidence as being wildly improbable and not worth further investigation, then I would submit that he is being willfully ignorant. I am at a loss to see what difference there is between willful ignorance about a minority group in a society and prejudice toward that group.

CHAPTER 4

Residual Biases

A principal argument for the persistence of anti-Catholic nativism is the systematic underrepresentation of Catholics in prestigious positions in society and the systematic lack of attention to that underrepresentation. The evidence of ignorance and residual bias I have said is confirmatory and persuasive. If a minority group is systematically underrepresented and you don't care about that underrepresentation; if you are ignorant of the facts about the social, political, economic, and attitudinal state of the group; and if you continue to use old stereotypes to organize your impressions about the group; then you may be fairly said to be bigoted against that group. To take a simple case: if you are either unaware of or unconcerned about the underrepresentation of Italians on the faculty of The City University of New York, if you are ignorant of the fact that there is now a substantial pool of Italians with doctoral degrees who could be added to the faculty of that university, and if you persist in thinking of *The Godfather* as a novel about a "typical" Italian, or Baretta

47

and Delvecchio as "typical" Italian cops, then an Italian might be excused for suspecting that you are an anti-Italian bigot.

Catholic underrepresentation and inattention to it can be proved with statistical evidence. Ignorance and residual biases can be illustrated only anecdotally, and those anecdotes cited in this chapter are offered as nothing more than anecdotal evidence. I think, however, that with a sufficient number of anecdotes, one can raise questions that challenge the society to at least confront the issue of anti-Catholic nativism.

I shall have to single out the *New York Times* with some frequency in this list of horror stories. I do so not because the *Times* is a bad newspaper but because it is the best newspaper; I do so not because the men who run the *Times* are my enemies but rather because I consider them my friends (and I hope I don't lose them by this book); I surely do not believe that the *New York Times* is an anti-Catholic journal—any more than I believe the University of Chicago to be an anti-Catholic university (though both institutions have some anti-Catholic staff members). Rather, I would insist that in the collective unconscious of the *Times* there are residual biases which, as good journalists and good Americans, the staff of the *Times* should strive to extirpate. I don't see them doing it.

ITEM: A reader wrote to the *Times* saying that the Catholic church (meaning me) should not talk about anti-Catholicism until it had purged the anti-Semitism from its own liturgical services. The reader went on to describe in heartrending detail how embarrassed he had been when he was invited to attend the confirmation of the son of a friend of his and discovered that there were anti-Semitic references in the confirmation service. The friend, we were assured, was also acutely embarrassed. Not having been to any confirmation services in the revised liturgy (some reflection on just how far out I am on the margins of the clerical culture), I had to dig up a copy of the ceremonial from a friendly bishop. I could find not the slightest trace of anti-Semitic reference. I sent my copy of the service to the editor of the *New York Times,* pointing out that I couldn't find anything anti-Semitic in the service and wondering if he could. If there were no anti-Semitic references, I said, it seemed to me that this ought to be acknowledged, for the *Times,* in printing a letter that stated what were in effect lies about the Catholic service, had helped to propagate, however unintentionally, a falsehood about a major American religious denomination. I got my booklet back in the mail sometime later, but there was no letter of response and no correction was ever printed.

ITEM: During the Roman Catholic Eucharistic Congress in Philadelphia, the *Times* (August 2, 1976) published a picture of Cardinal Sheehan, the retired archbishop of Baltimore, sleeping in the middle of one of the liturgical services. I wrote to both the editor and the publisher of the *Times* to suggest that the picture was in poor taste; I wondered whether the *Times* had ever in the past or would ever again print pictures of black ministers, Anglican bishops, or Jewish rabbis sleeping during a

49

religious service. The publisher did not reply, but the editor did. He agreed that the picture was in bad taste and admitted that he was shocked to see it, but he rejected my assumption that there was any particular anti-Catholic bias in it. I responded by reiterating my list of minority religious leaders, asking whether the editor really thought that a photographer would snap any of them in such circumstances, whether the picture editor would select it for publication if he had, and whether the page editor would print it. I received no reply. As Jimmy Breslin has said, "It really isn't anti-Catholic, it's just the way things happen to work out at the *New York Times* newspaper."

ITEM: The daily book review in the *New York Times* carries a headline, "When Irish Eyes are Riling." So I read the review and send this letter to the reviewer:

September 13, 1976
Dear Mr. Broyard:

Let me begin by saying that for a long time I respected you as one of the most perceptive book reviewers in America—and this was even before you were kind enough to say some kind things about books of mine. Hence, if I write a letter of mild protest, the reason is not so much to harass you as because I have committed myself to a systematic one-man campaign against stereotyping of the Irish, and I don't figure I can stop simply because a reviewer has been good to my books.

As you may have guessed by now, my objections are to your review of Edna O'Brien's *Mother Ireland*. [*New York Times*, September 1, 1976] You quote with apparent approval

50

Edna O'Brien's comment that the Irish "are at home with blood. Their history and mythology drip with it." Now I've got to say to that, Mr. Broyard, "Oh, come now!"

The last time Ireland engaged in aggressive warfare was in the fourth century. Ireland is the only country in western Europe where conversion to Christianity involved no martyrdoms, no forced converts, no bloody battles. Since that time the Irish have gone forth from their boundaries always in peace; and from the time of Columkille on through several centuries they brought peace and order to western Europe ravaged by Dark Age invasions. With the exception of the draft riots in New York and the 1919 riot in Chicago, the Irish political history in the United States, for weal or woe, has been one of compromise and coalition building— indeed, much to the offense of those who prefer their politics to be ideological. The Irish presence at the UN has always been one of peaceful moderation. Most serious historians will tell you that the modern Irish nation emerged not so much from the 1916 revolution and civil war but from the peaceful nineteenth-century tactics of O'Connell, Davitt, and Parnell. Ireland is the only new nation in the twentieth century to have developed a successful functioning two-party system; and in that system the losers of the civil war, within a decade after it, replaced the winners in political power by a peaceful elective process.

There has been a lot of blood shed in the last 1,000 years of Irish history, most of it Irish blood and mostly caused by foreign invaders—according to some tabulations, as many as 7 million murdered under British tyranny from the time of Elizabeth I to Elizabeth II. It is not the Irish who are a bloodthirsty people but those who invaded and oppressed her.

51

You may argue that you were merely citing Ms. O'Brien and not personally subscribing to her positions, but I would reply by saying that if a Jewish writer argued that Jews were dishonest businessmen, or a black writer wrote about the laziness of blacks, you would have promptly disassociated yourself from such stereotypes. It seems to me to be appropriate to expect you to disassociate yourself from stereotypes about the Irish.

"Ah," you say, "but Ms. O'Brien is an artist. She is painting her own picture of Ireland, a highly personal one; and no claim is being made that it has sociological accuracy." I would respond in roughly the same fashion as previously stated. If a black or Jewish writer presented degrading stereotypes of his own people, the American cultural and intellectual elite would fall over itself rejecting such stereotypes. Why is the self-image of the Irish acceptable? And I suppose I don't have to add, by the way, that Edna O'Brien's writing is self-hatred? Her view of the Irish is stereotypical.

Finally, those familiar with Irish historiography would, I think, advise you not to begin reviews with Girald of Cambrensus—even if Ms. O'Brien chooses to use such quotes. Good old Girald was a paid historical hack of the English, writing a biased and unfair story about the Irish precisely to justify continued English oppression. He ought not to be taken seriously as an objective reporter of the facts of the Irish life of his time.

But I have the terrible feeling that Girald of Cambrensus, if he were alive today, would receive rave reviews in the *New York Times*.

I hope our paths cross sometime during my pilgrimages to the *New York Times'* building so that we can discuss this and other matters. Let me repeat what I began with: your reviews are one thing I never miss in the daily *Times*.

Cordially yours,
Andrew M. Greeley

Now I get a lot of crank mail for things I write, and, let me tell you, a letter like the preceding one would be in the upper one-tenth of one percent for courteous, pleasant, friendly disagreement. I would certainly respond. Mr. Broyard didn't.

ITEM: The *Christian Century* (April 14, 1976) published a long editorial review about a social science study of American Catholics. The editorial writer describes a number of questions that the respondents in the study are alleged to have been asked. He then dismisses the findings and advances his own explanation for the changes in Catholicism in the last decade. One would never know from reading his editorial that his scenario had been tested and found wanting; nor would one know that the questions allegedly proposed by the survey interviewers were not in fact on the instrument. Since the *Christian Century* offices are in Chicago, it doesn't take a long-distance toll to call them; so I phoned the editor and said that I had helped to design the questionnaire and the study and couldn't find the items that we were alleged to have asked. Would he be so kind to point them out for me? He admitted that I might have a legitimate complaint and suggested I write a letter, so I did. It took three months for the *Christian Century* to get around to publishing it, and, of course, they didn't apologize.

ITEM: In an article in the *New York Times* about California's governor, Jerry Brown, Richard Reeves observed that the Jesuits teach that the end justifies the means—one of the oldest canards in the history of bigotry.

53

In other articles Reeves often referred to Catholic congressmen as hacks—Peter Rodino and Thomas O'Neill being the most recent to receive the appellation.

ITEM: Professor Morton Kaplan of the political science department of the University of Chicago, in commenting upon his accepting an invitation to the Reverend Sun Myung Moon's intellectual festival in New York City, noted that he saw no difference between what Reverend Moon preached and Roman Catholicism.

ITEM: The Rockefeller Foundation gave a very large grant to the American Jewish Committee to interpret Catholic ethnics to the intellectual world—without bothering to give any similar grant to a Catholic group. Dr. John Knowles, president of the foundation, was astonished that Catholics would protest.

ITEM: Kenneth Vaux writes in the *Christian Century* (March 5, 1976, p. 213): "The trial [*Massachusetts v. Edelin*] took place in South Boston, where the Catholic ethnic community is strong. The white, predominantly male jury was drawn from this populace so recently disgraced by a commingled racial and religious animosity generated by school integration and busing." Later in the same paragraph he says, "Those who have been victimized now victimize others with a vengeance."

I would object to Vaux's statement on a number of grounds:

(1) The Suffolk County Courthouse, where the trial took place, is in Boston right off Beacon Hill; it is not in South Boston. The regional adjective is not only inaccurate, it is a deception (perhaps unconscious). It

54

links in the mind of the reader the Edelin trial with the school busing controversy. Whether Vaux did this deliberately or not doesn't much matter; he clearly reveals the cast of his own attitude.

(2) The jury panels that serve Suffolk County are drawn from the entire city of Boson (and Revere and Chelsea). There is no reason to think that many of the jurors came from South Boston. To say that they were drawn from a community "recently disgraced" by "racial and religious animosity" is completely gratuitous in the absence of specific proof that the jurors did indeed come from this district.

(3) Those who served on the jury may well have had antibusing opinions, but the fact that some Catholics in the Boston area are against busing does not mean that all Catholics are against it. After all, it was a Catholic judge who ordered busing.

(4) Nor does it follow that even if they were against busing, the Catholics on the jury would be unable to suspend their feelings on that issue while making a decision about the Edelin case. As far as I can recall, the *Christian Century* has not suggested that the Watergate jury (mostly black) was punishing the Nixon aides for that administration's racial policies. Blacks in Washington apparently can suspend their sense of being victimized; Catholics in Boston cannot.

(5) It is at least an open question about who is disgraced by the busing controversy, the Catholics in Boston or the suburbanites who are able to run from city problems and leave the poor and less well-educated whites

to pick up the tab.

ITEM: Syndicated columnist Marquis Childs writes about the "Hail Mary-praying" Catholics of South Boston who oppose busing. He does not feel constrained to add that the suburban judge who imposed it on the poor people of South Boston but not on his own suburban enclave is also Irish Catholic and presumably says the Hail Mary himself on occasion (as does the NAACP lawyer in the case, himself an Irish Catholic).

ITEM: The official interpreters of American Catholicism in the national media are all individuals who have departed in one way or another from the mainline Catholic community (Wills, Sheed, Harrington, Robert Sam Anson, Pete Hamill, for example). Robert Sam Anson's article in *New Times* (May 17, 1974) on Irish power in the church (which ignored the fact that Boston's bishop is Portuguese, Brooklyn's and Cincinnati's are Italian, and Philadelphia's is Polish) would hardly have been printed if it had been about blacks or Jews. And can you image *New York* magazine using a statement like Hamill's proud boast that the "new Irish" (whoever they are) think like Jews if such a self-hating sentiment had come from a black? What would happen if Polish jokes were told about Chicanos?

ITEM: In her response to those who had the temerity to criticize her antiabortion plot article in *Harper's* (June 1974), Marian Sanders says that from the grammar and syntax of her critics it is clear that the writers are not regular readers of that magazine. And Hunter Thompson, in his freaked-out account of the McGovern loss, usually throws the word "Catholic" into his litany of unpleasant adjectives about Thomas Eagleton.

ITEM: Robert Pirsig writes in a review in the *New York Times Book Review,* "I hope, for his own sake, that his final choice [of a new wife] is someone who really appreciates him for the good man he is." Preferably, Pirsig says, it should be an "Eastern, Polish, Roman Catholic woman, heavy boned and big breasted, domineering and authoritarian, from a childhood of poverty.... She should love him earthily and also her children and her church." Pirsig tells us that for the Catholic layman morality is external, that for Catholics the "other-directed authoritarian system of moral education" becomes the pattern of life, and that Catholics are moral weaklings by the standards of Protestantism.

A colleague said, when I complained about the utter silence of the various libertarian and antidefamation organizations on this review, "But isn't what he said about Polish Catholics true?" This is like asking a black if it isn't true blacks have a natural sense of rhythm and a peculiar smell, or like asking a Jew if it isn't true Jews are less honest in business than other people.

ITEM: No national newspaper or television network maintains a regular correspondent in the Republic of Ireland or in northern Ireland. There are more Irish-Americans (three times as many) than there are Jews, yet correspondents are sent to Jerusalem but not to Belfast or Dublin. I have no objection to correspondents' being in Jerusalem—they ought to be there—but they ought to be in Belfast and Dublin, too. Maybe then we would not get such terrible coverage from that part of the world.

ITEM: As far as I am aware, there was no editorial comment and very little coverage in major American newspapers of the condemnation of Great Britain by the European Court of Justice for its use of torture in Northern Ireland. The oldest democracy in the western world was guilty of using torture against political prisoners, and the American media ignored it.

ITEM: A young American mother who was visiting Ulster was stopped at a checkpoint by British soldiers, beaten into unconsciousness, and thrown into a jail. No charges were made against her, no crime was committed; she was eventually released, but there was no protest from the American government, and no notice was taken in the American press.

ITEM: Orde Coombs wrote a vicious attack on Daniel P. Moynihan in the *New York Times* Op-Ed page, charging him with wanting to keep blacks trapped in slavery and in devotion to the Virgin Mary just as the Irish were trapped. Leaving aside the gratuitous falsehood of the charge against Moynihan, one wonders how the *Times'* editors allowed in print such a blasphemous attack on a religious symbol of one-quarter of the American population.

ITEM: A nun at an American state university who sought a master's degree reports the following to me about her professor:

My teacher spent long hours and even mentioned in my class

[history of psychology] that the Catholic churches in the Middle Ages are symbols of repressive political power. He claims today that the Pope threatened to excommunicate Catholics in Italy if they voted communist even though the communists promised not to bother the church. He claims the church is supporting the Christian Democrats who support capitalists. . . . He asks why is it that the Pope is always Italian. He points out that many nuns who've left the church because they were "oppressed" have come to the state school psychologists and to him and wept and agonized in paroxysms of guilt are symptomatic of the church.

Can one imagine a professor at a state university using academic freedom and the taxpayer's money to perpetrate such a gross assault on any other denomination or minority group in the nation or the society and getting away with it? But Catholics are fair game, it seems, particularly for academics who claim to be Marxist.

ITEM: An Italian graduate student at Yale University tells me that several faculty members delight in ridiculing Italians when there are Italian students present. It's all very genial and sophisticated, of course, not gross and stupid in the manner cited above. Yale is the place, you remember, where, when Mario Procaccino announced he would run against John Lindsay for mayor of New York, a faculty member said, "If there is any people who is inferior, it has to be the Italians."

ITEM: On December 7, 1976, the day before the Feast of the Immaculate Conception, the *New York Times* Op-Ed page published an article by Marina

An Ugly Little Secret

Warner (the author of *Alone of All Her Sex* [New York: Knopf, 1976]) bitterly attacking the Catholic cult of Mary and claiming that both humanity and the dignity of women had been severely harmed by that cult. Later, when the *Times* found itself inundated by letters complaining about the publication of such a piece on the eve of the Feast of the Immaculate Conception, it reported its regrets "for any offense this inadvertent timing may have given to our readers" and assured the readers that it was an "unfortunate and entirely accidental coincidence."

The Op-Ed page is, of course, an appropriate place for discussion, and the *Times* is perfectly within its rights in printing Ms. Warner's column—even though Garry Wills, of all people, in the weekly book review, had effectively destroyed the credibility of *Alone of All Her Sex.* But one wonders why the *Times* did not publish a scholarly column on the other side of the issue, a possibility that seems not to have occurred to the Op-Ed page editors. The editors' claim that they didn't know that December 7 was the eve of an important holy day for one-quarter of the American population was not only not any excuse at all, but one more gratuitous insult to American Catholics.

ITEM: The 1977 film *Nasty Habits,* based on a novel by Muriel Spark, is alleged to be a satire on Watergate, but in fact it is a scurrilous attack on Roman Catholic nuns. John Simon, writing in *New York* magazine— hardly a journal noted for its support of Catholics— wondered about the public outcry if it were the Black

Muslim religion which had been so mercilessly satirized.

ITEM: The Catholic League for Civil and Religious Rights has done a study of the history textbooks used in public schools and finds that such textbooks invariably emphasize the poverty, ignorance, and stupidity of the immigrants and their Americanization by the public schools. Virtually none of the textbooks even mentions the existence of Catholic schools.

ITEM: In a suit filed in the United States District Court for New Jersey against certain forms of state aids to Catholic schools, Leo Pfeffer, of the American Jewish Congress, charged that Catholic schools are racially segregated and that help for Catholic schools from the state of New Jersey promoted racial segregation—this despite the fact that Mr. Pfeffer knows as well as anyone else about the tremendous influx of non-Catholic blacks into Catholic schools not only in New Jersey but all over the country. He also ought to be aware of the fact that 75 percent of children in Catholic schools are in schools which are in fact racially integrated.

ITEM: In a review of a book by Susan Cahill called *Earth Angels* (New York: Harper and Row, 1976) in the *New York Times Book Review* for November 28, 1976, the reviewer, Jane O'Reilly, says that the remarkable scenes in Susan Cahill's book are not satire: "Thus, for example, she describes a nun calling the role of the freshman class, 'Maria Mannion. Mary Donoghue. Margaret Murphy. That's a good Irish name, Margaret. I taught your brother at All Martyrs. Nina I...Io...I-o-dola? Another good Irish name, get that hair back off your face.

Martha Girlinghosen. I had your sister in Flushing. Wipe that smile off your face. Mary Anne O'Connor. You're the scholarship from St. Joan's. We'll be watching you.'" O'Reilly adds, "The repressions and processions, the intellectual evasions, the spirit-breaking meanness could never be reconciled with Faith, Hope and Charity. . . . the consolations of the Faith could never console us for the classroom." No nuance, no qualification, no suggestion that things might be different elsewhere. That's the way it is with all nuns and all Catholic schools apparently. One wonders whether the *Times* would print such bigotry in its book review section if any other religion were the object.

The list could go on endlessly, quite literally ad nauseam. Either the point has been made sufficiently by now, or the reader has long since dismissed me as a demented paranoid. But I think that the fact that these things could happen in America in the middle 1970s at least raises the question of whether a deep-seated anti-Catholic animus still remains among those who report on, interpret, and think seriously about what goes on in the country.

My case remains what it always was. The real proof of bigotry, I think, is not that these things happen, but that they go unnoticed.

CHAPTER 5

Ethnicity, Catholic Schools, and the Educational Enterprise

I n this chapter I propose to speak about two subjects that have occupied my research concerns for the better part of the last decade and a half—"white ethnics" and Catholic schools. I intend to suggest that the reaction of the upper levels of the American educational enterprise to both subjects has been shaped in great part by anti-Catholic nativism, not to say racism, and that while this prejudice exists today in more sophisticated form, it has scarcely diminished in scope and intensity from its virulent manifestations earlier in this nation's history.

I shall use the term "American educational enterprise" repeatedly in these remarks. Let me clarify what I mean by it. First of all, I don't mean school teachers or principals necessarily; I mean upper-level school administrators, professors and deans of education (particularly of the better education school faculties), editors of educational journals, educational writers for the national press, state and national educational bureaucrats, foundation executives, and professors of social sciences and the humanities at the major elite American universities. I do not mean that *all* such people respond to the subjects of ethnicity and Catholic schools with nativist racism or that even a majority of them do; but I propose to suggest that a very substantial minority is heavily influenced, albeit unconsciously perhaps, by anti-Catholic attitudes and thought.

To my first point. Four extraordinary events occurred in the American republic in the first three decades of the present century: the "noble experiment" of Prohibition, the First World War, the Spanish influenza epidemic, and the immigration of over ten million foreigners, mostly eastern and southern European Catholics, between 1900 and 1914 (during each of five years in that era, more than one million immigrants poured into the country). The First World War and the "noble experiment" have now become nostalgic memories; the Spanish influenza epidemic we repressed deep into the unconscious until the outbreak of swine flu at Fort Dix (though perhaps some of my own generation, whose parents almost died of it and who heard terrifying stories about it in our childhood, remember better). But the vast immigrant movement and the intense nativist reaction to it in the 1920s, so much a part of our very recent history and so important in shaping the contemporary American social structure, is something that, for the most part, we pretend simply didn't happen— save for occasional reference to the "wretched refuse." For some odd reason, the offspring of the wretched refuse have been known not to like the phrase.

But let me describe a neighborhood to which some of these people flocked:

> The neighborhood is a ten square-block area with almost 14,000 people, an average of 39.8 inhabitants per acre—three times that of the most crowded portions of Tokyo, Calcutta, and many other Asian cities. One block contains 1,349 children. A third of the neighborhood's 771 buildings are built on "back lots" behind existing structures. The buildings are divided into 2,796 apartments with a ratio of 3.7 rooms per apartment. More than three-quarters of them have less than 400 square feet, 556 are in the basements in which tenants stand knee-deep in human excrement when the plumbing breaks down in even moderate rainstorms.
>
> Garbage disposal was a chronic problem—usually it was simply dumped in the narrow passageways between buildings. The death rate was 37.2 per thousand. Nine thousand of the neighborhood's inhabitants used outdoor plumbing. The people there were the poorest of the poor, making less than three-quarters the income of nonminority group members in the same jobs. Desertion, juvenile delinquency, mental disorders, prostitution were the highest in the city there; social disorganization in this neighborhood, according to all outside observers—even the sympathetic ones—was practically total and irredeemable.[1]

Now good, solid, respectable American citizens were disturbed by the poverty and suffering in that neighborhood called "the Stanislowowo" (after Saint Stanislaus Kostka, its parish church). But they did not conclude, as many would conclude a half century later when they saw other such urban ghettos, that the poverty in the Stanislowowo was the result of injustice and oppression. Rather, they believed that the people's condition there was their own fault. They were ignorant, illiterate, inferior, and there was not much hope of their ever becoming good Americans. If they continued to pour into the country, heaven only knew what terrible things would happen to American society. And so the infamous Dillingham Commission was set up to recommend a response to the immigration "problem." Among other things, the commission told the people of America that the eastern and southern European immigrants were racially inferior. Italian immigrants were "innately criminal" and Polish immigrants had racially "unstable temperaments" which made for family crisis and disorganization. The task of "Americanizing" such immigrants would be staggering; laws had to be passed quickly to prevent any more from entering the country. And they were indeed very quickly passed.

After the racism of the Dillingham Commission, the cultural disorganization theory advanced by the Chicago School of Sociology (of which I am, in some fashion or another, an illegitimate and rejected offspring) offered a relatively more benign explanation of the poverty and suffering in the Stanislowowo. The immigrants were not racially inferior but merely culturally inferior. In *The Polish Peasant in Europe and America* (a study of the very neighborhood described above), it was explained that the poverty and misery were a result of the confrontation between an old-fashioned medieval peasant culture and a modern scientific urban culture. The problem,

then, was not so much to keep the immigrants out—
though, of course, that had to be done too—as to assimilate and "Americanize" those who were already here. A
study of the Americanization campaign of the 1920s has
yet to be done. We eagerly study what nineteenth-century
American racists did to the Indians but pay no attention
at all to what twentieth-century American racists tried
to do to eastern and southern European Catholics. However, it is clear from even casual references in the literature
of the era that the Americanization campaign was based
on the assumption that the eastern and southern
European immigrants were either racially or culturally
inferior and that it was the mission of all institutions
in society, and especially the public schools, to turn this
"wretched refuse of the earth" into something approach-
ing modern Americans.

Some of the most distinguished American educators of
the first decades of this century—progressive intellectuals
all—were totally committed to the concept of the racial
inferiority of the immigrants. Men like E. A. Ross, Henry
Pratt Fairchild, and John Commons insisted that democracy was a monopoly of Anglo-Saxon, Nordic, and
Teutonic groups and that it was intrinsically impossible
for other cultural groups to attain it. Even Robert E.
Park of the Chicago School, surely no racist, insisted
that "assimilation is thus as inevitable as it is desirable. . . .
If we tolerate their strangeness during their period of
adjustment . . . then we hasten their assimilation."

Understandably, some of the immigrants didn't like
this. A fair number of the people in the Stanislowowo

67

were able to read English and some were able to respond to what the Chicago School had to say about them. But curiously enough, such responses never seemed to find their way into the University of Chicago sociology bibliographies.

The social work and social service administration types, as well as educational administration types, all over the country were heavily influenced by the Chicago School; in their turn, they doubtless influenced many of the New Deal social reforms. You help people to over-come inferior cultures, it turned out, by tearing down their neighborhoods and destroying their family life with a welfare program that made it profitable for fathers to leave the home. Fortunately for the Poles, they were beyond the reach of such reforms by the time they became effective. Ironically, just across the river from the Stanis-lowowo is the Cabrini Green housing project, one of the ugliest and most evil things human good intentions ever put together—a monument to public housing and to welfare legislation. I suspect that the Poles and the Italians got out just in the nick of time.

But the notion that public education had a mission of Americanization went hand in hand with the well-intentioned but counterproductive New Deal social reforms. As recently as the 1950s, James B. Conant, that distinguished American educational theorist, was ar-guing that everyone simply had to go the public high school, because it was to be the institution which would form a common culture for all Americans.[2] The sons and daughters and grandsons and granddaughters of the

68

eastern and southern European immigrants were to learn how to be as American as everyone else in the public high schools.

A word should be said in passing about the Irish, most of whom were here before 1900. There was not much doubt in anyone's mind among those in the educational enterprise that the Irish were culturally inferior. They were superstitious, hard drinking, sexually inhibited, contentious, colorful, erratic and unpredictable—that was Paddy for you. And in the cartoons of the nineteenth century, he was often portrayed as an ape with a shillelagh in one hand and a stein of ale in the other. The stereotype persists; one can even find it in some books written by Irish Americans, such as Moynihan's essay in *Beyond the Melting Pot* (Nathan Glazer and Daniel Patrick Moynihan [Cambridge, Mass.: MIT Press and Howard University Press, 1963]) and William Shannon's study, *The American Irish: A Political and Social Portrait* (New York: Macmillan, 1974), where it is assumed that unfortunately the Irish have never quite been able to make it out of the lower middle class. Perhaps the principal difference between expectations about the Poles and Italians as opposed to expectations about the Irish is that there was some hope for Americanizing the former; the Irish were no good altogether, and even some of their own began to believe it.

The myth of the cultural inferiority of the Catholic ethnic has persisted into the present, although it has gone through some interesting transformations and transmutations. In the 1950s, it was the Catholics who

69

were supposed to be the backbone of the radical right. After all, wasn't Senator McCarthy an Irish Catholic? (There was a later Senator McCarthy, but we never seem to get any points for him.) After all, weren't the Lithuanians and Poles so furious at what had happened to their native countries that they all became rabid anticommunists? (Jewish support for Israel is fine; Polish support for freedom in Poland is somehow or the other right-wing and un-American.) It was generally assumed then, and I think it is generally assumed now, that Catholics were disproportionately among the supporters of the first Senator McCarthy and the anticommunist witch hunt. From being considered not patriotic enough in the 1920s, they had mysteriously come to be seen as too patriotic.

The superpatriot of the 1950s was converted into the white ethnic-hard hat-racist-chauvinist-hawk of the 1960s and 1970s so dearly beloved by professors, educators, editorial writers, clergymen, TV commentators, reporters, and national columnists. Everyone knew, you see, that Catholics—still disproportionately blue collar—were more likely than other groups to favor the war in Vietnam, to vote for George Wallace, to be part of the white racist backlash, to support Richard Nixon, and to be against radicals, drugs, college professors, women's libbers, and all the other contemporary folk heroes. The white ethnic and his counterpart, the middle American, were the scapegoats of the 1960s and the 1970s. You had to blame someone, you see, and Jews and blacks were no longer fair game; so the old nativist prejudice against the ethnics, never really exorcised, was called back into play. As a result of the ethnic backlash, it is imagined by a substantial proportion of America's intellectual and cultural elites (to say nothing of the leadership of the educational enterprise) that there is also an ethnic "revival" or an ethnic militancy. The hard hats out there in the streets are apparently ready to rise up in resistance to all of the things that have happened in American society since 1965. Racially and culturally inferior, un-American at first, then superpatriotic, and now ethnic racist reactionaries—that is the sad history of the children, the grandchildren, and even the great-grandchildren of the turn-of-the-century immigrants. There is, after all, relatively little progress from the dumb Polacks of Nelson Algren's novels and the Stanley Kowalskis to the Don Corleones. And the Irish, represented as they are by Richard J. Daley, Daniel P. Moynihan, and George Meany, are as inferior as ever.

There are, of course, some facts available. I despair of repeating them because no matter how richly documented they are, no one seems to believe them. However, for the record, let me make the following observations:

1. The eastern and southern European immigrants now have a higher college attendance rate than the national average for young people of college age. They made little progress during the nativist 1920s and the Depression 1930s, but in the space of a single generation, between 1945 and 1970, Poles and Italians have surpassed the national average in college attendance. (The Irish, incidentally, also surpassed the national average, and

71

they did it in 1910. In fact, we poor, semiliterate descendants of Europe's oldest culture are now more likely to go to college than Episcopalians—though we are seldom deemed bright enough to be college presidents.)

2. Holding constant all pertinent regional, city-size, and educational variables, eastern and southern European immigrants not only earn more money than the national average for whites but also earn more than British Protestants. Those who could not assimilate have become successful. Indeed, within the space of a generation they accomplished what people said they could not possibly achieve. Irish Catholics, for example, are the richest, the best educated, and the most occupationally successful of any Gentile group in American society. And in terms of income at least, the Italian Catholics are right behind them—and moving up fast. I know that is impossible; it is true nonetheless.

3. Furthermore, the ethnics made it into American society while maintaining many of their distinctive cultural patterns. The reformers didn't, after all, manage to Americanize us in the public schools; and that, peculiarly enough, did not turn out to be a barrier to our advancement. On the contrary, there is substantial evidence that it is precisely the strong values of home, family, and neighborhood that facilitated the educational, economic, and occupational success of the ethnics. And how is it that they became successful? The full story of the ethnic miracle cannot be told yet, and given the reluctance of agencies like the Department of Health, Education, and Welfare to fund research on ethnic groups, it may never be

told. But there is a strong hint that they made it through the good, old-fashioned virtues of thrift, industry, and hard work. In 1905, in the city of Chicago, when vast numbers of Poles were just barely off the boat (and some of them still on it), 15 percent of the money in Chicago's savings and loans were in Polish-owned institutions. It was at about that time that a University of Chicago observer complained about the Chicago Italians—"All they're interested in is making money." How dreadfully Protestant of them.

4. There is absolutely no evidence in the research done on the radical right (for example, see the work of Seymour Martin Lipset) to indicate that Catholics were disproportionately numbered among the supporters of Senator Joseph McCarthy or the anticommunist witch hunt. I know evidence does not make myths go away; nonetheless, that's what the evidence says.

5. Catholic ethnics are less likely to be "hard hats" than others, and the term "blue-collar ethnic" is no longer an appropriate description of what is typical in the ethnic groups. However, there is also evidence that during the Vietnam war, in the city of New York, three weeks after the famous Wall Street demonstration, construction workers were the occupational group most likely to oppose the continuation of the war. Catholics were more likely than the national average to be against it from the beginning; they were less likely to vote for Governor George Wallace (in the 1968 election, Jews, Poles, and Irish were the white ethnic groups in the country—in that order—most likely to vote for Senator Humphrey); and on

a wide variety of measures of social and political liberalism, Catholics—particularly the Irish—are left of center rather than right of center. Ethnics are also less likely to score higher on measures of racism than the average even in cities in the North.

I could go on, but the point is made, I think.

Insofar as we have any empirical evidence, it not only fails to confirm but also positively refutes the white ethnic stereotype; yet I would contend that this stereotype is the most powerful and most pervasive inkblot in American society today and is fundamentally irrefutable—largely because it reveals more about the emotional needs of those who propagate it than it does about the personalities and political beliefs of those whom it alleges to describe.

One nice thing about the white ethnic-racist-chauvinist-hawk stereotype is that it justifies making the ethnics the fall guys for social reform. As long as court-ordered social engineering is to be used to right the racial wrongs of the past, and as long as such social-engineering decisions are limited to the central cities, then it will inevitably be those members of the ethnic working class who remain in the city who will pick up the costs of appeasing other people's consciences. They will expiate for racial injustices they never created and from which they have benefited very little. Judges in Newton can play games with inner-city schools and judges in Flossmoor can play games with inner-city housing without paying any attention to the fact that suburbanites are essentially parasites, living off the economic, industrial, and labor base of the cities, but

74

escaping—through the legal fiction of city boundaries—
from the problems and the costs of urban life.

What, then, are the charges that can be made against the
American educational enterprise on the subject of anti-
Catholic nativism?

1. Public education was deeply involved in the racial
and religious bigotry of the Americanization campaign
of the 1920s and 1930s. It has never acknowledged its
responsibility for such a campaign and is, I suspect, even
now not ready to admit that it was wrong. We expiate for
what we have done to the blacks and Latinos, but not for
what we have done to the Catholic ethnics.

2. The American educational enterprise has paid very
little attention to the heritages and the experiences of the
ethnic collectivities—on the general assumption, apparently, that these heritages in both their Old World and
New World manifestations are inferior, mediocre, and
second-rate, as they were called in the *New Yorker*. (See
Naomi Blivon, "E Pluribus What?," *New Yorker* 47
(November 20, 1971): 225-26, 228-29.

3. The American educational enterprise has acquiesced
in the white ethnic-racist-hawk myth and has done little
to contend with that myth despite overwhelming empirical evidence that disproves it.

4. The higher educational enterprise continues to
propagate the myth of Catholic intellectual inferiority.
There is always considerable concern about the underrepresentation of blacks and women in educational
institutions, but no discernable concern about the absence
of Catholic ethnics. If one raises the question of why

there are no practicing Catholics in the social science faculty of a distinguished American university, one is told that the Catholic religion is a barrier to intellectual eminence. There is lots of empirical evidence to refute this assertion, but it doesn't seem to do much good.

5. There is in the educational enterprise an almost complete silence about both the immigration experience of the first two decades of the century and the nativist reaction of the second two. Nor does there seem to be much serious intention to break the silence. While there are a considerable number of younger scholars and graduate students who are doing research on ethnic subjects, the principal public and private funding agencies (with the exception of the National Affairs Division of the Ford Foundation) have systematically refused funds for basic historical, sociological, anthropological, and psychological research on ethnic diversity and on the ethnic miracle of economic success without cultural assimilation. There is the Ethnic Heritage Studies Act, which HEW did not want and which proceeds on the curious assumption that you can find educational resource materials without first doing basic research. The program, however, is clearly tokenism with a vengeance, a sop thrown to the ethnics to keep them quiet. Whenever one attempts to persuade a funding agency that the study of white ethnics in America is a legitimate and necessary scholarly pursuit, one runs the risk of being told that one's work is antiblack.

6. Despite their educational and economic achievements, there is still systematic discrimination against

eastern and southern European Catholics in the occupational world, a discrimination almost entirely limited to those who have attended college. Our evidence shows that the discrimination against eastern and southern European Catholics is some 40 percent of that directed against blacks. Discrimination against blacks is well known, acknowledged and contended with in American society; discrimination against ethnics is ignored. Yet one need only look at the foundation offices in New York, at the educational research agencies in Chicago, at the national media, at the arts and sciences faculties of distinguished private universities, and at the education schools to realize that the presence among them of a practicing Roman Catholic is indeed a rarity. Research carried on by the Institute of Urban Studies in Chicago shows that Italians and Poles are only a tiny minority of corporate board members in that largely ethnic city. If the same finding had been reported about blacks or women, it would have received national publicity—and it would have deserved to. But when it is Poles and Italians who are underrepresented, Americans take it to be a matter of course; and there is nothing in the behavior of the American educational enterprise to challenge that nonchalance.

The ethnics are not suffering. Economically they are doing substantially better than the average and substantially better than their ancestors would have believed possible. There are not, despite Michael Novak, millions of militant ethnics out in the streets ready to begin a crusade. Why should there be? They like America; they've never had it so good. It is, however, precisely among the well-educated ethnics, those who might aspire to make it into the intellectual and cultural elites, that the protest is rising and will continue to rise and grow in the years ahead. It is the ethnic graduate student who will not turn against his heritage to please the arrogant young professor who ridicules it who is likely to turn militant; or the ethnic intellectual who finds that the experience of his family is not an appropriate subject for literature or art or scholarship in the United States while the experience of other people's families somehow or the other is; or the ethnic scholar who finds that being a publicly practicing Roman Catholic is still a barrier to a successful academic career. The Kennedy election seems to have eliminated much of the grass-roots nativism in American society, but the subtle, sophisticated nativism of the intelligentsia persists.

Then there is the matter of the Catholic schools. They emerged as a reaction first of all to the Protestant orientation of the common school in the nineteenth century and then to the nativist orientation of the public school in the twentieth century. They were, according to Dr. Conant, an obstacle to Americanization and to the creation of a common culture. They were divisive. Fortunately, we are told, Catholics are becoming disenchanted with the schools, and we can cheerfully expect that they will vanish from American society.

Still, it must be noted that the Catholic schools have emerged as an exercise of the thoroughly American right of freedom of choice and that this exercise has been bitterly opposed by most professional educators,

academics, and the elite of the educational enterprise
for the whole of this century. They have made little
effort to find out what happens in the Catholic schools
or to measure their impact. The American educational
enterprise has damned them as second-rate, inferior,
un-American, divisive, and the result, to use Mr. Justice
Powell's charming words, of ecclesiastical discipline.
The American educational enterprise does not know
much about Catholic schools, but it knows that it is
against them.

There are research findings that show that the schools
are not divisive, that they have facilitated economic and
academic success for their graduates in America, that
American Catholics are as committed to them as they
ever were and believe that their schools would receive
state help were it not for anti-Catholic prejudice. Indeed,
there is evidence that 90 percent of American Catholics
favor the continuation of such schools, that 80 percent
would contribute more to the Sunday collection to keep
the schools open, and that there is as much as 1.8 billion
dollars of potential untapped support for parochial
schools in the Catholic population. There is also, incidentally, evidence that Catholic school attendance
leads to lower scores on measures of racism and anti-
Semitism, and there is no evidence that it leads to any
less interaction in adult life with members of other
religious denominations. If Catholic school attendance
has declined, the principal reason is that the American
Catholic hierarchy, in a characteristic loss of nerve, has
not built schools to keep pace with the suburban

migration of Catholics. Do not console yourselves, gentlemen, with the thought that this single significant alternative to the monolithic monopoly of public education will go away; it will be around for a long time to come.

But there has been another exercise of educational freedom of choice in recent years over which the American educational enterprise has discreetly spread a veil of silence: black parents, in ever increasing numbers, are making substantial financial sacrifices to send their children to Catholic schools. I estimate that in the city of Chicago, one out of every ten blacks is in a Catholic school, and that half or more than half of these students are not Catholic. It would appear on the basis of National Catholic Education Association (NCEA) data that black enrollment in Catholic schools goes up every year despite the decline in total enrollment, and that it goes up anywhere from seventy thousand to ninety thousand students a year—most of them non-Catholic.

This is an extraordinary phenomenon. Inner-city black parents, most of them Baptist or Methodist, are, at the cost of considerable personal financial sacrifice, sending their children to Catholic schools rather than to public schools. I, for one, would like to know why. But if there has been any attempt on the part of the national, state, or local educational bureaucracies to understand the reasons for and the effects of this exercise of freedom of educational choice, it has escaped my attention. In fact, most people in the educational enterprise discreetly pretend that it isn't happening or make comments about how Catholic schools can expel their problems and public schools can't and how when the brightest black kids go to Catholic schools, that leads to a deterioration of the atmosphere in public schools. One hears these comments but never sees any data indicating that there are massive expulsions of unruly children from Catholic inner-city schools (there are not, incidentally), or that the departure of some students from the jungles of inner-city public education has made things any worse than they already were there.

The implications of the exercise of such freedom of choice are massive for the American educational enterprise. Could it be that the muscle-bound, overbureaucratized, strife-ridden, slow-moving, rigid, unresponsive public education bureaucracy is perceived by an ever-increasing number of black parents as incapable of dealing with their children's educational needs? Could it be that the increasing demands for educational freedom of choice would suggest that, far from being the wave of the past, alternatives to public education are the wave of the future? Indeed, could it be that we would already have a much broader freedom of choice in the American educational enterprise if it were not for the fact that it would be terribly difficult to exclude Catholic schools from such an educational reform? Could it be that we will never have educational reform in the large cities of the United States until we break up the public educational monoply? And could it be that one of the main reasons why the public educational monoply has not been seriously challenged yet is that potential challengers

81

are afraid of doing anything that might benefit the Catholic schools?

Minimally, one has to admit that the Catholic schools are an interesting phenomenon and that their survival among the well-educated and financially successful Catholic ethnics and their new attractiveness to inner-city blacks suggest that they just might be worth more study. How can it be that the per pupil costs of Catholic schools seem to be about $1000 a year less than the per pupil costs of public schools? I guess I get a little suspicious when I am told that that's because the Catholic schools don't run programs for handicapped children. How come the educational bureaucracies of Catholic schools are so small? How come there is so much local control? How come so many schools are quite literally administered by elected parish school boards without, be it noted, much chaos and confusion? How come, with less money and less bureaucracy by way of input, there is a much higher academic output in the Catholic schools? One hears, of course, that they get the best students. But why do parents of the best students choose to send them to Catholic schools? These are interesting questions, surely, and while one might speculate on the answers, I would submit that to date we have no answers at all to these questions and no indication that anyone is particularly interested in finding them. Yet I must note that if any institution other than the Roman Catholic church were providing such a massive educational alternative for blacks in the inner cities, the praises of that institution would be sung loudly up and down the length and breadth of the land.

I must also note that our leaders deserve no credit for the existence of the inner-city Catholic schools that serve mostly non-Catholic blacks. We stumbled into this educational alternative largely because we were too inept and too stupid to close down the schools quickly when Catholics left the neighborhood. However, in a number of cities, most notably my own (Chicago), the gloriously reigning bishops are now determined to phase out the schools, arguing with marvelous Christian insight that they have no obligation to provide schooling for non-Catholics. That the schools are kept open now at all is the result not of hierarchical vision—of which we have very little—but of courage and vigor and sacrifice from the lower clergy and the laity.

And, so I wonder. Where are the research projects funded by the federal, state, or local governments, or by the large private funding agencies? Where are the research programs in the schools of education around the country? Where are the scholars on the education faculties, particularly at places like Harvard and the University of Chicago, who specialize in studying Catholic schools or the relationship of ethnics to American education? The answer is that there aren't any, there aren't about to be any, and one is a damn fool for even thinking there would be.

Our proposal to the National Institute of Education for the study which resulted in the recently published *Catholic Schools in a Declining Church* was cut to 40 percent of its original budget—just enough to fund the

83

data collection. I asked the project officer how the rest of the effort was to be financed. "Oh," he said casually, "the church will pay for it." I must say that I think that such ignorance of the actual situation is every bit as bad as the refusal of the dunderheads who currently lead the American Catholic church to do any research on their own. So the study was done in our spare time and with funds cribbed in various ways that need not detain us here. I just wonder, however, if NIE would have said the same thing to someone who was doing a study of black or Spanish children.

(In addition to the tremendous increase in black enrollment in inner-city Catholic schools, there has also been a considerable increase in Latino enrollment. While such families come from a Catholic tradition, that tradition has never taken parochial schools seriously, and the shift of ever increasing Latino population into Catholic schools is every bit as impressive an exercise of freedom of choice for the Latins as it is for the blacks.)

Is the nativism of the American educational enterprise conscious and deliberate, or is it unconscious? I suppose the best answer to that is to point to the people who say, "But isn't Catholicism really an obstacle to independent intellectual activity?" That's about on the level of asking, "Isn't it really true that blacks have a distinctive body odor?" Or, "But isn't it really true that Polish and Lithanian Catholics are more likely to vote for George Wallace?" I would submit that such questions have much in common with such remarks as "Isn't it really true that Jews are more likely to cheat at business?" or "Isn't it really true that women are happier at home raising children?'' The person who asks the question may not realize that he is a bigot, but he is still a bigot.

CHAPTER 6

Catholics and Jews

The following paper was commissioned by the American Jewish Committee to be read at its annual meeting in 1976. It was carefully screened by a number of Jewish colleagues and by the staff of the AJC. The reaction to the paper at the meeting itself was mixed but mostly positive. However, after the meeting there was a very hostile reaction from many people, a reaction which seemed to be based primarily on incomplete reports and excerpts. I reproduce the paper here in the exact form in which it was given so that the reader may judge for himself how "anti-Semitic" it is. When people ask me, "Why single out Jews when it is a wider problem?" I answer that I "singled out" Jews (insofar as I did) because a Jewish agency asked me to.

WHAT HAVE YOU DONE FOR US LATELY?

Let me begin by saying that while I am wearing a Roman collar and sporting my defiant shamrock, I am in no sense speaking as a representative of the hierarchy or of the Catholic church. On the contrary, I have the distinct impression that a substantial proportion of Catholic church leadership would be delighted if I went away and never came back. Unlike my friend Mr. Michael Novak, I make no claim to speak for millions of either Catholic ethnics or Irish. Thus I represent no more than a constituency of one.

But that never kept an Irishman quiet before.

I propose tonight to make six general observations about Catholic-Jewish relationships in the United States and then refer to five specific "flashpoints."

My first general observation is that it seems to me that on the basis of both the data and my impressions, the general relationship between American Catholicism and American Judaism is excellent—perhaps better than the relationships between the two historic offshoots of the Sinai religious tradition are anywhere in the world. With the exception of New York City, the excellence of this relationship ought to be the context of our reflections. No other comments I make in the course of the evening should be interpreted out of that context. I said, "except New York City" advisedly, because there is, I think, something potentially very unpleasant in Catholic-Jewish relationships in the New York metropolitan area. I am not a New Yorker, I have never done research on the subject, and I do not trust my impressions sufficiently even to detail them tonight; but it may well be that you have a critical problem in that area.

I would also add that as far as I can see, there is no decline in the overwhelming Catholic support for the American alliance with Israel. My impression is that that support is not based on the moral excellence or justice of Israel's cause (and it would be a mistake for you gentlemen to appeal to that motivation) but is based on the fact that Americans admire the spunk and modernity of Israel and support it strongly because such support is something their Jewish fellow Americans still want very much. Would such support survive another oil embargo? No nation would be wise to try to blackmail the United States of America for very long; they would find it to be extremely counterproductive.

Secondly, I would observe that some of the most exciting scholarly work being done anywhere can be found in the historical, archaeological, and theological rediscovery of the Second Temple era. It seems to me that in this rediscovery scholars are uncovering linkages and connections between the two descendants of Second Temple Judaism that no one would have dreamed possible just a short time ago. Without going into the details, one can now say, I think with some confidence, that Christianity and Judaism, as they exist today, are quite clearly offsprings of the same fundamental religious traditions and of the same critical religious era we call the Second Temple. Such an insight does not mean that the two offsprings are about to merge, but it does mean that they have far more in common than was previously thought. Indeed, one could go so far as to say that there are some aspects of the Second Temple era and experience that are perhaps better preserved by its contemporary Christian offspring than they are by the contemporary Jewish one. Such a subject is beyond my scope tonight; I simply want to note and take encouragement from the remarkable scholarship being done by researchers of both heritages in this decisively important period of human history.

Third, I wish to comment that it seems to me when we

speak of "Catholic-Jewish relationships," we engage often in the fallacy of misplaced concreteness. For there is no such thing as one Catholic or one Jewish community. Among the six million American Jews and the fifty million American Catholics, there is a wide plurality and diversity of viewpoints, interests, commitments, values, and goals. Some Jews and some Catholics may be locked in angry combat, but it would be a mistake to see that as typical of Jewish-Catholic relationships or to generalize from it to the existence of very serious problems between the two communities. I do not suggest that such combats may not be serious—some of them are; but I am suggesting that they are not necessarily legitimate bases for more generalized diagnosis. Thus there is doubtless an acute conflict between the Catholic Right-to-Life movement and abortion groups which have many Jews in their membership. The Right-to-Life movement is not representative of American Catholicism, despite its claims to be, and I presume its adversaries who happen to be Jewish are not representative necessarily of Judaism either. The abortion conflict is indeed going on between some Catholics and some Jews, but it is not a conflict between the two communities and I think should not be defined as such.

Fourth, there is emerging in America a "communal Catholic," that is, a Catholic who is loyal to his tradition and heritage—even proud of it—but who does not take the clergy or hierarchy seriously as intellectual, political, moral, or social leaders. You will not be able to understand American Catholicism unless you realize how powerful this tendency is.

Fifth, while generally there are good feelings between the two communities, I am compelled to report that a number of different data sets available to me indicate that pro-Catholic feelings among Jews have declined in the last decade while pro-Jewish feelings among Catholics have either held steady or increased. Hence, at the present time, there seem to be stronger pro-Jewish feelings among Catholics than vice versa. Our data sets do not enable us to explain this change or even to hazard a guess as to what implications it might have for the future. My own personal hunch is that it may be part of the more general phenomenon of scape-goating Catholics that I think has been going on in American society for some time now. It is not a specifi-cally Jewish phenomenon. I would urge, as I have urged before, joint research by representatives of both com-munities on the subject. (I also think there ought to be joint research on the rather acute problem which I per-ceive to exist in New York.) I do not expect this joint research to be undertaken, but I would be lax in my responsibilities if I did not urge it at least.

Finally, I am impressed by the importance of the stylistic differences among American religio-ethnic collectivities. I think all of us for too long bought the melting pot-assimilationist view of things and just assumed that cultural diversity would go away. In fact, many of the differences persist—some major, some minor—among the ethnic groups in American society; and some of these even minor differences turn out to be aggravating and important without our even being aware of the fact that they are at work. If we have abandoned the assimilationist perspective—and I take it we have—then we must be much more sensitive to the stylistic cultural differences. We must strive to understand them, enjoy them, and to prevent them from prohibiting our conversations and our common work. Let me be more explicit.

Three of the differences that I can talk about I think have been pretty well documented by our research. Jews and Irish Catholics (to take two groups at random) are very different from one another in their approach to expressing affection for children, drinking, and in their political participation. The differences are not universal; there are many Irish who don't drink and I suppose there are some Jewish alcoholics, though I have never met any. But an Irishman who believes that a relaxing evening is not possible without the drink-taking and a Jew who is disgusted by anyone who takes more than one drink are going to have a very powerful hidden agenda in their interaction unless they are quite self-conscious about the origins and the nature of these differences. It is not necessary, incidentally, to say that the other style is as good as mine; it is enough to understand why it is different. (Let me add that in this particular area, I am much more likely to be on the Jewish side than the Irish.) Similarly, while Jewish affection for (and anger toward) children are explicit, direct, and forceful, the Irish expression of affection is much more likely to be indirect, circumlocutory, and passive. It does not mean that the

Irish love one another or their children any less than Jews, but that we have very different ways of showing it. The Irishman with a Jewish neighbor is likely to be deeply offended by what he takes to be the emotional self-indulgence of the Jewish parent, while his neighbor is likely to be appalled at the Irish coldness with their children. Again, one must make major efforts to avoid value judgments on these subjects and take them into account in our common work and conversations.

Finally, the data show that the typical Polish and Italian approach to solving a civic problem is to call one's precinct captain or one's brother-in-law (who may, incidentally, be one and the same person), while the Jewish and Protestant tendency is to summon a community meeting and form a civic organization. The Irish, hyperactive political types that they are, are likely to engage in both behaviors. The tendency for Jewish and Protestant types to dismiss the personal-contact approach to politics as old-fashioned and possibly corrupt is, I think, very strong. So, I suspect, would be the Polish and Italian propensity to think the "civic" approach is stuffy, self-righteous, and moralistic. The Irish propensity to think that putting all of your eggs in one participative basket is dumb may well be the strongest tendency of all. Unless we are aware of these stylistically different approaches to political participation, we may misunderstand thoroughly what the other is about.

There are other differences which I cannot document with data but about which I have very strong impressions. First of all, the matter of communication: the Catholic ethnic in general, the Irish Catholic in particular, is prone to indirect, circumlocutory, informal, and soft-spoken communicative style. The Irishman, for reasons having to do, perhaps, with the Penal Times, is reluctant to give a direct answer and much prefers to answer a question with another question or to respond not verbally but with a shrug of the shoulder, a wink of the eye, or absolute silence. The Irishman is likely to make a request very casually and indirectly. The English phrase, "would you ever . . . ?" (as, "Would you ever come to Washington to give a talk?") is the translation of a Celtic phrase which has escaped me. It represents, I think, the strong cultural tendency of the Gaelic linguistic tradition to avoid sharp or abrupt communicative styles. There are no swear words in Gaelic, for example, and when a modern Irish-speaking person wishes to swear, he falls back on English words. Indeed, the language does not even have a word for "hello" or "goodbye." One enters the house and says, "Peace be to this house"; when one leaves, one says, "Jesus and Mary be with this house." One meets someone on the street and says, "Jesus and Mary be with you"; the response is "Jesus and Mary and Patrick be with you." (Presumably, in the pagan days there were appropriate deities used in their place.) The Jewish communicative style, as I understand it and as I have experienced it, is rather more direct, to put the matter mildly. My sister, the theologian, works at De Paul University with two Jewish colleagues (which is a whole other story altogether). She remarked to me once that she felt she had a very difficult time making her Jewish colleagues understand the problems she was experiencing in the environment. I told her, "What you've got to understand is that there are two Jewish ways of talking—loud and louder. Shout at them and they'll hear you." With some effort she learned to shout and now things are much better. Similarly, not so long ago I was having a minor altercation with one of my colleagues at NORC. Not having had much sleep the night before, I did a very rare thing and started to shout at him. He beamed; his eyes lit up, his mouth expanded in a great warm smile. "You're shouting at me," he said with delight. "You're damn right I'm shouting at you!" "How marvelous!" he rejoiced. "You know, in all the years you've known me, this is the first time you've shouted at me."

The idea that shouting at a person could be a compliment until then had escaped me completely. I quickly pointed out to him the important social psychological fact that it takes a lot for an Irishman to work up enough anger to really start shouting, but then when he does, he's likely to remember it for twenty years.

This is anecdotal, of course, though I gather that a lot of people can match the same anecdote. It is a difference about which we must know and understand much more, it seems to me, if we are to get along well with one another. I also have the impression that Jewish political and social action is powerfully influenced by guilt rhetoric. I sometimes have been appalled at the highly exaggerated appeal to guilt and personal responsibility for various world problems. In fact, it has always seemed to me that the issues, while serious and demanding great personal concern, hardly involved any personal guilt. I didn't cause it not to rain in the Sahel, for example. The guilt rhetoric seems to be effective with people inside the Jewish community. It is, however, usually counterproductive with the Catholic community, particularly the Irish Catholics. You can appeal to fairness, justice, decency, and generosity with a Catholic audience, but don't try to make us feel guilty for things we did not do personally because it turns us off very quickly. The Irish, for example, may feel guilty at having let mother down; indeed, that is a burden of guilt we carry through our lives (I have the impression from some Jewish novels that that may be one of your problems too), but that is about the only kind of guilt we do feel. Our social guilt is minimal. Mind you, you can get us to be socially generous, but I am suggesting it's a mistake to use guilt to motivate us. It won't work.

I would urge that these and similar stylistic differences are of very considerable importance, that we do not know nearly enough about them, and that they ought to be the subject of joint research. I don't think this research will occur—at the risk of repeating a now familiar theme—but I think it ought to occur.

Let me add hastily that these stylistic differences are matters of degree. There are indirect, soft-spoken Jews and loudmouthed, direct Irishmen, God only knows. But I would at least offer to you as a plausible hypothesis for further exploration that differences in communicative style may be rather more important than we had previously thought.

I now turn to five specific flashpoints. They are not areas where I expect major crises, but they are areas of potential or actual misunderstanding that can occur between individuals and groups. It occurs to me that some of you may well be offended by the points I am about to make. For that I am sorry, because I have no desire to give offense. On the other hand, Rabbi Tanenbaum asked me to come to speak the truth; honesty compels me to say that from the Catholic viewpoint, at least from the viewpoint of this Catholic constituency of one, these are problems—not great big hairy ones, but nonetheless problems of some importance to which attention should be paid.

Let me note very carefully before going on to discuss these flashpoints that I am not speaking about "Jewish traits." I am speaking about behavior that goes on in America's cultural and intellectual elites, some of which is Jewish. I am not saying that all Jewish intellectuals or even a substantial minority engage in the behavior I am about to describe. Nor am I saying that only Jewish intellectuals engage in such behavior. I am saying rather that there are flashpoint problems when some Jewish intellectuals—probably a small minority—engage in behavior which many non-Jewish intellectuals also engage in.

I do not see how I can say it any more clearly. I will grow upset if anyone persists in misinterpreting what I shall now say.

First of all, the white ethnic, blue-collar, racist, hard-hat, chauvinist, hawk image has become a favorite whipping boy for the national media, elite and popular. One

97

needs someone to hate, someone to blame for what is going wrong in society, and since it is no longer legitimate to blame blacks or Jews, the "Middle American" and the hard-hat ethnic have become favorite targets. This Catholic ethnic inkblot was not created by Jews; indeed, the American Jewish Committee's Ethnic America project has vigorously resisted it. Nonetheless, many of those of both the university and the media world who propagate it are Jewish, and one has the impression that some of them rather enjoy flailing away at the white ethnic bigot. Some Catholics are sophisticated enough not to equate a given Jew who is propounding the ethnic stereotype with Judaism; others are not, particularly when the stereotype looks like an attack on Catholicism as such. There may be a substantial amount of educational work to be done within the Jewish community to make it clear that the stereotype is not only demonstrably false but also counterproductive.

Secondly, there is still substantial discrimination against Catholics, particularly practicing Catholics, at the upper levels of America's elite culture. In the national media, certain governmental agencies, many if not most of the great national foundations, and the finest elite universities, discrimination against Catholics is rife. It is justified by the viciously bigoted argument of Catholic intellectual inferiority, an argument which simply does not admit of refutation even if you have overwhelming data to disprove it. Again, Jews did not create this discrimination and, in the case of the foundation world, are probably almost as much victims of it themselves as are Catholics. Nonetheless, it must be said in all candor that some Jews aid and abet it and continue to propound the myth of Catholic intellectual inferiority. One is hard put to see very many Jews, who have been so vigorous in their criticism of racism and sexism, raise much in the way of objection to anti-Catholic nativism. As more and more younger Catholics begin to move into this world of the intellectual and cultural elites and discover, as Michael Novak did, how strong the nativist biases are, they will be offended when they see some Jews propounding nativist bigotry and practicing nativist discrimination. Some of the more sophisticated may well be able to distinguish between what individual Jews do and Jewish traits and propensities; others may not. I could easily make a case that my problems at the University of Chicago were almost entirely the result of machinations of anti-Catholic Jews. The case would be true, although I would also have to add very quickly the fact that almost all of my friends and supporters at the University of Chicago were also Jews who were astonishingly pro-Catholic. I do not think every Catholic who tries to claw his way into the world of the upper academy will be able to say that.

Third, many of the new generation of Catholic ethnics who are now showing up at the best graduate schools of the country are no longer disposed to take a stand of apology and shame over the past and their own heritages. They don't really feel inferior; they don't feel that being Polish, Italian, or Irish is second-rate, mediocre, or anything of which to be ashamed. When they learn from

99

a bright, arrogant young faculty member that the conventional wisdom of the liberal upper academy views them and their people with scarcely veiled if unintentional contempt, they are not likely to accept it. There was a generation of Catholic would-be intelligentsia who for one reason or another thought that the only way to make it in the academy was to deny their pasts, their heritages, their religion. They found, as Michael Novak did, that even then they couldn't make it. But the present generation will not go the self-abasement route; on the contrary, they will fight back. And when that smart, arrogant, articulate, self-confident junior faculty member turns out to be Jewish, he runs the risk of stirring up needless anti-Jewish sentiment. Again, one can easily argue, and I would completely agree, that it is not only Jews who propound the stereotype of Catholic cultural inferiority, and by no means do all Jews do so—indeed a majority of Jewish academics do not. I am simply saying that when a Jewish scholar does this to a Catholic student, one has a flashpoint situation.

Fourth, there is a propensity for many non-Catholic scholars to ignore the impressive economic and educational achievements of American Catholics. In fact, our recent research on their achievement, I think, has generally been pooh-poohed if not dismissed by many non-Catholic social scientists. The Poles and Italians, obviously an inferior people, simply couldn't be as successful as the NORC data claim they are. May I say that those are fighting words? More particularly, I think there is a strong tendency among many Jews to ignore, deny, or

minimize the immense importance of the contribution
that the Catholic parochial schools have made to the
success and self-confidence of the ethnic immigrants.
They overlook completely the fantastic popularity of
the inner-city Catholic schools among members of the
black community. Black enrollment in Catholic schools,
most of it non-Catholic, goes up year by year as much as
seventy thousand or eighty thousand students. It is the
only educational alternative, the only option for freedom
of choice available to most inner-city blacks. Candidly,
such a service deserves not to be ignored. Presumably we
do not expect and will not get gratitude from the Jewish
community for this important social service, but it is
time at least to end the pretense that the service is not
occurring. I disagree with the content, the tone, and the
timing of Cardinal Krol's complaint about Jewish opposition to Catholic schools; and yet I think I understand
the feeling. I think that much opposition to Catholic
schools is in fact anti-Catholic, and I note that the certi-
fied, liberal, card-carrying Jewish intellectual Adam
Walinsky thinks the same thing. (See Adam Walinsky,
"Aid to Parochial School," *New Republic*, October 7,
1972, pp. 18-21.) I am not prepared to say how much of
the interminable hectoring about separation of church
and state is crypto-bigotry, but some of it surely is; and
the nasty, vicious tone of the opposition leaves little
doubt that there is more at stake than constitutional
principles.

It is, by the way, worth observing that the correlation
between Catholic school attendance and the absence of

anti-Semitism is even stronger than it was when we did our first study ten years ago. There seems to be no more effective way of reducing anti-Semitic feelings than to support Catholic schools. But then that was clear ten years ago, too.

In fact, the real enemies of Catholic schools are not their opponents within the Jewish community but the Catholic hierarchy, which has lost its nerve. There is, as our recent research shows, more than enough money and willingness to spend it in the Catholic communities to sustain and indeed expand the parochial school system. Cardinal Krol is shifting the blame away from those who ought to bear it when he attempts to blame Jews for the decline of Catholic schools. Quite apart from the question of state aid, one must simply say that one has the impression that a very substantial number of American Jews hate and despise Catholic parochial schools—and systematically ignore evidence about their positive benefits. I will not attempt to explain the reasons for this hatred (I suspect in part it is simply a hatred of Catholicism as such), but tonight I simply wish to make the point that given the strong and, indeed, as our evidence shows, undiminished Catholic enthusiasm for such schools, confrontation between the strong Catholic support of what we think of as "our" schools and the strong animosity that many (though I dare say not most and certainly not all) Jews feel toward the schools is surely a potential flashpoint in our relationships.

Finally, I wish to say something about the very delicate issue of reciprocity or, more concretely, about the issue of "what have you done for us lately?" An increasing number of American Catholics are beginning to say, "We have gone down the line more than once with you on support for Israel and for freedom of Soviet Jewry. When are you going to do something for us in return?" We have been told in response, indeed, we have been told by Rabbi Tanenbaum, that issues of Israel and Soviet Jewry are issues of such surpassing moral excellence that they are simply not subject to barter, negotiations, and deals. I must candidly say that I think such a response does not indicate sensitivity to what is being said. No one is suggesting that we do a straight player trade, Israel for parochial schools. What I am suggesting is that when a relationship begins to be perceived as a one-way street by some of the people in it. there are potential trouble spots.

To put the matter even more bluntly. Why is it that all Jewish issues, and only Jewish issues, are of surpassing moral excellence? Why is it that all of our issues are relatively less important and seem to make no major claim at all on moral concern? Justice for the people of Israel is supremely important, but justice for the Catholics in the nasty little colonial regime in the north of Ireland is not. Freedom for Soviet Jewry is of capital concern, but freedom for the Catholic captive nations is not. One is told that Ulster is a very complicated problem and that political realism demands that one give up any hope for liberation of the captive nations. Complexities and realism affect our issues, but not yours. I begin to wonder why. I was told once, after addressing

103

(for free) an audience of Jewish women, that the world had a moral obligation to support Israel to expiate for the holocaust. No such moral obligation existed for the Catholic cause in Ulster. I asked her if she had ever heard of the potato famine, and she said no, she had not.

I might also note that I rarely if ever hear it mentioned that many of the peoples in the captive nations suffered holocausts of their own in the early 1940s. Apparently that gets them no points for their cause.

The reciprocity issue is doubtless a complex one, and it is not yet a serious flashpoint if only because there are not very many of us who have worked long enough in Jewish agencies to have become disillusioned by the fact that loyalty and friendship seems to mean one thing to us and another to you. Granted that this is an understandable difference in style. I would merely submit that it may be a critically important one in years to come.

On the most general level of reciprocity, I should like to politely wonder when American Jews, to modify slightly the question of Norman Podhoretz, will face their "Catholic problem." There is strong and powerful anti-Catholic feeling in the Jewish community. The empirical evidence shows it, the impressions of many Catholics indicate it, and not a small number of Jews will acknowledge it—though usually off the record. Yet this problem has never been faced publicly and dealt with. Not all, not a majority, not even a large minority of Jews are anti-Catholic; yet some are—unless you wish to argue that Jews alone of humankind are free from bigotry. I think that Catholics have acknowledged the

104

existence of anti-Jewish feeling in the last years since the Council and have worked against it—though perhaps not effectively enough. As far as I can see, there has been no reciprocity at all from the Jewish side. I wonder if there ever will be.

Catholics have studied their own anti-Semitism. Jews, as far as I know, have not studied their own anti-Catholicism. I have been monitoring anti-Jewish attitudes among Catholics for ten years (they keep going down). I am unaware of any Jewish scholar who has been monitoring anti-Catholic attitudes among Jews.

CHAPTER 7

The Catholic Nonresponse

T hose who are most to blame for the persistence of anti-Catholic nativism in the United States are the Catholics themselves.

The reason that most Catholics are not concerned about anti-Catholicism is that they are not hurting. To put the matter concretely, Italians may be somewhat unhappy to know that they are only 5 percent of the faculty at CUNY while being 25 percent of the student body; they also may be unhappy that Italians who live in the poor neighborhoods of the city have become targets for positive discrimination campaigns from which suburbanites are immune. But most Italians are not candidates for faculty positions at CUNY and do not live in neighborhoods threatened with some mad bureaucratic or judicial scheme for expiating the sins of the past. On the contrary, most Italians are doing quite well in American society; they have the second highest family income of any white gentile group in large cities in the North, and they are, if truth be told, breathing down the necks of the Irish as the highest paid white gentile group

in the country. You may sympathize with the Ph.D.'s or
the people in the poor neighborhoods, but the poor can
move and the scholars can get jobs working for the
federal government. So who suffers?

I could insert "Poles," "Irish," or any other white
ethnic group in the paragraph above as the operative
proper noun. People simply do not become militant
when they are leading the good life. Anti-Catholic
nativism was not a sufficiently powerful barrier to prevent the ethnic immigrants, their children, and their
grandchildren from becoming economically successful.
So who cares about it?

So the *Village Voice* blasphemes the Virgin Mary;
Time and *Newsweek* make abortion "the Catholic issue";
there are virtually none of us working for the Rockefeller
Foundation; the *New York Times* prints pictures of
sleeping cardinals; and there are few Catholics on the
faculties of Harvard and Yale. Who cares? For Catholics
the schools are there, the church is there, and they continue to improve their economic position in American
society. The hell with the nativists!

It is a reasonable position. Mayor Daley was reelected
every four years despite the pleas of liberal reformers
that blacks should make alliance with the Jews instead of
with the "corrupt Irish"; Daniel P. Moynihan wins a
senate seat in New York with three-quarters of the black
vote despite the liberal opposition. So what does it really
matter what the nativists think? Catholics have learned
to live with them and to avoid the occupational careers,
the magazines, the newspapers, the academic environ-

ments where they are likely to encounter nativism.

There are a few people who are concerned about the captive nations and a few who are concerned about Northern Ireland. Both groups are furious about the lack of interest in government and intellectual circles in these two horrendous examples of oppression; they are equally furious that the national media either pay no attention to them or report them inadequately and inaccurately. But most Irish really don't care much about Ulster, and most Poles, Lithuanians, Slovaks, and Hungarians are only marginally interested in the captive nations. They have their jobs, their families to raise, the next weekend to look forward to. America has been good to them—very good indeed—and to hell with the double-domed ivory-tower intellectuals.

More than that must be said. The successful Catholic middle class is distressed by militancy. Its members do not want to become associated in the public mind with kooks, crazies, misfits, troublemakers, and malcontents. They do not want to be identified with the nutty blacks, pushy women, sick homosexuals, and other weird people who spew forth their anger and their hatred on the television screen. Protest is not respectable; it is part of the crazy counterculture of the 1960s that the ethnics found intensely offensive. They'll be damned if they'll stoop to using such techniques. Maybe if the shoe were pinching; but it isn't. For example, most Catholics find the militancy of the more strident antiabortion activists to be an acute embarrassment, not because they support abortion, not even necessarily because they oppose

109

legislation against abortion (though the majority of
Catholics do *not* support a constitutional amendment
against abortion); they are embarrassed by the placard-
waving, picket-line-marching antiabortionists because
they are uneasy with demonstrations of any kind. "Don't
those people," asks the typical Catholic, "have anything
better to do?"

Nor are there any Catholic community leaders who
are willing to do active battle against nativism. The
bishops are overwhelmed by the administrative responsibilities of their own dioceses and by the mushrooming
responsibilities of the complex and muscle-bound
national heirarchy, which, with one or two exceptions,
is served by incompetent staff offices. The internal
politics of the Conference of Bishops and the need to
keep Rome happy impel the bishops to adopt stances and
take positions that are ill conceived and often irrelevant.
Discrimination against working-class Catholics through
"positive discrimination" and intellectual Catholics
through occupational discrimination are matters of
which the bishops are only dimly aware. They perceive no
advantage in terms either of Roman approbation or of
recapturing influence over their own rank-and-file in
taking a serious interest in either subject.

Catholic union leaders and Catholic politicians, who
in an earlier era handled the political and civil side of
Catholic upward mobility while the clergy and hierarchy
handled the religious side, are not especially concerned
about issues of cultural politics; they view themselves
as the representative of all their constituencies rather

than of their Catholic and ethnic supporters. It is perfectly legitimate for a black political leader to speak mainly for blacks (until he becomes the head of a multiracial coalition); but an Irish political leader—already likely the head of a coalition—can hardly be expected to speak just for Irish constituents or just for Catholic constituents. The newer generation of more self-conscious and active ethnic leaders has yet to acquire major clout in either political organizations or the trade unions. So as the political game becomes more and more one of assigning quotas to various minorities, neither the civil nor the religious leadership is particularly interested in making sure that the quotas do not discriminate against Catholics. They are under no pressures from their large and happily satisfied middle-class constituencies to be concerned about such problems.

Catholic social-action leaders, who once were close to their own people, have now largely turned against them and written them off as "Archie Bunkers" (a term used at the "representative" meeting of American Catholics in Detroit during the bicentennial year). Archie Bunkers, you see, don't have any rights, and if they are discriminated against, it serves them right. If they converted from their racism and expiated their sins, maybe the Catholic social activists would be concerned about them again—but don't bet on it.

For the same reason the leading Catholic journalists, writing either for the Catholic press or for the secular press, find the subject of nativism embarrassing. For if it has persisted and you have paid no attention to it, then somehow or other you may have sold out your own kind either to present the fashionable liberal party line in your Catholic journal or to achieve career success in the world of secular journalism. It is precisely those Catholics who have made it who are most eager to deny the existence of discrimination, because if they have made it despite discrimination, then it might appear that they have paid the price of soft-pedaling their Catholicism, which some of them most certainly have done.

And, of course, there are points to be made with the important reference groups by attacking those who raise the question. Hence, Rev. Charles Angell (in a letter to the *New York Times*, November 10, 1976) and Rev. Edward Flannery (two Catholics specializing in dialogue with Jews) jumped all over me when I suggested that there might be some anti-Catholic feeling among a few Jews. Flannery argued (in the *Chicago Tribune*, October 23, 1976) that Jews had the right to anti-Catholic feeling because of twenty-three hundred years of Catholic persecution. (Though the Catholic church is only some nineteen hundred years old.) He never did answer my question as to whether the Irish had the right to anti-English feeling because of seven hundred years of English persecution. So I presume that in Flannery's peculiar vision of morality, bigotry becomes justified only after a thousand years of persecution.

For denying the existence of anti-Catholicism both gentlemen earned lots of points and received many kudos from the important reference groups, which are not Catholic, of course. There are, you see, no points to be earned at all for attacking anti-Catholicism.

So we have the paradoxical situation in which there is a good deal more concern among both Protestants and Jews about the persistence of nativism than there is among Catholics. There are a number of reasons, it seems to me, for this phenomenon.

1. Protestants, Jews, agnostics, and others who are offended by anti-Catholicism encounter it more frequently than Catholics do because of the circles in which they normally move. If you are at gate 14 at a Notre Dame game at half time, who the hell cares what's being said in the Harvard and Yale faculty clubs? But if you are in the Harvard or Yale faculty club, you might at least notice, if not care.

2. Genuine liberals, the non-Catholic opponents of nativism, simply do not think it is a good thing for any kind of bigotry to persist in a society. True to their own principles, they reject nativism every bit as much as they reject anti-Semitism, racism, or sexism. They may not be quite ready to venture into public print to attack it, but they at least will deplore it privately and urge Catholics to begin to do something about it. And if a Catholic does begin to do something about it and gets clobbered in the pages of the *New York Times,* they may even write letters of protest—which usually don't get published.

3. The non-Catholic antinativists also see a much more serious problem coming down the turnpike as more and more younger Catholics begin to pursue careers in the arts, the sciences, and the professions that will inevitably

113

bring them up against the barriers of nativist bigotry. They are aware, for example, of the fierce tensions beneath the surface in New York City and of the strong possibility of Catholic (mostly Italian) conflict with Jews in that city in the years ahead. They realize that almost any Italian conflict with Jews will lead to Italians being charged with anti-Semitism, but they also realize that name-calling will not solve the conflict.

Nativism is not merely a bad thing in itself: it is potentially a serious danger (though scarcely a fatal one) for the American pluralistic experiment. The conflict, these observers know very well, could get much worse in the years ahead; for just as the new Catholic intelligentsia is becoming more and more restless with the nativism it encounters, the rest of society's elites are searching for a new scapegoat to blame for the things that have gone wrong. They can no longer scapegoat blacks or Jews, so guess who that leaves.

My guess is that they are right, that there is potential for conflict ahead. I do not propose to exaggerate this potential—the society will not be torn apart by religious conflict (though New York City might be). Too many Catholics are doing too well, too many ethnics have become too successful to take militancy all that seriously— barring some economic cataclysm. Neither a minor problem nor a fatal one, conflict generated by nativism could still become a nasty phenomenon in our country in the years ahead.

These Protestant, Jewish, and agnostic enemies of nativism maintain an anxious silence and only egg foolhardy people like me on to do battle with the nativists. "Raise the consciousness of your constituency," they say in effect, "and if your people make enough serious demands, we will attempt to lead a positive response." It is a not unreasonable stance to take. Those who opposed racial discrimination in the United States were only really able to do something about it when the civil rights movement of the late 1950s and early 1960s raised the consciousness of blacks.

I therefore conclude this volume on a melancholy note. Nativism persists, it is likely to continue to persist, and it may just cause serious problems in the years ahead. It will be extirpated only if a sufficient number of Catholics become deeply concerned about it, and the likelihood of that is not very great.

And what about you, gentle reader? Have I raised any doubts in your mind? Do you now begin to wonder why American social science has for more than three decades virtually ignored the possibility that nativism might persist? Do you think that there are grounds for at least a preliminary exploration into the parameters and dynamics of anti-Catholic feeling in American society? Should we take a closer look at it?

And if we shouldn't, why not?

Notes

CHAPTER 1

1. The statistical evidence to support these assertions can be found in my *Ethnicity, Denomination and Inequality* (Beverly Hills: Sage Press, 1976).
2. Kenneth R. Hardy, "Social Origins of American Scientists and Scholars," *Science* 185 (August 9, 1974): 497-506.
3. To say that Catholics have been successful in the academy in the last decade does not refute my previous contention that they are excluded from the top places in the intellectual establishment. Catholics are virtually invisible, for example, on the faculties of the great private universities such as Harvard, Yale, Princeton, Stanford, the University of Chicago, and there are few Catholic college presidents in America. The fact that Catholics have become successful in the various academic disciplines merely refutes the charge that they have not received the top positions because of some kind of Catholic intellectual inferiority.
4. For a full discussion of the article, see Cullen Murphy, "Turning Away From the Status Syndrome," *Change*, Vol. 6, No. 8, (October 1974).
5. Lavender and Forsyth, "The Sociological Study of Minority Groups as Reflected by Leading Sociological Journals," *Ethnicity* 3 (December 1976): 388-98.

CHAPTER 2

1. Allan Chase, *The Legacy of Malthus: The Social Costs of the New Scientific Realism* (New York: Knopf, 1976). Subsequent references in text are to page numbers from this edition.
2. John Higham, *Strangers in the Land: Patterns of American*

Nativism, 1860-1925 (New Brunswick, New Jersey; Rutgers University Press, 1955) and John Higham, *Send These to Me: Jews and Other Immigrants in Urban America* (New York: Atheneum Press, 1975); Edwin A. Moore, *A Catholic Runs for President: The Campaign of 1928* (New York: Ronald Press, 1956); Ray Allen Billington, *The Protestant Crusade, 1800-1860: A Study of the Origins of American Nativism* (Gloucester, Maine: Peter Smith, 1964).

3. John Higham, *Strangers in the Land.*

CHAPTER 3

1. The materials used in this chapter are discussed at much greater length in my book, *The American Catholic: A Social Portrait* (New York: Basic Books, 1977).

CHAPTER 5

1. Andrew M. Greeley, "The Ethnic Miracle," *Public Interest* 45 (Fall 1970): 20.
2. James B. Conant, *American High School Today* (New York: McGraw-Hill, 1959).

CHAPTER 6

1. Bertram Gold, of the American Jewish Committee, responding to the heavy pressures that were brought against me because of distorted versions of the speech printed here as chapter 6, wrote me the following letter to make clear that as far as the leadership of the American Jewish Committee was concerned, the paper was not "anti-Semitic." I include here my response to the letter:

    Dear Andy:
    It was good to see you at La Guardia Airport and to reminisce

with you about the work you have done with us over the years—all of which I have always thought to be professionally competent and responsible. It was also good to learn that despite the recent misunderstanding, as a result of your long relationship with us, you still have positive feelings towards AJC.

The public controversy over your paper at our annual meeting was most unfortunate. As you remember, many who were at the meeting reacted affirmatively to your presentation, feeling that it was a serious effort to examine a difficult, complex and challenging issue.

I am sure that most of the negative reaction afterward resulted from the reading of incomplete segments of your presentation. Surely no one who is familiar with your work could seriously question your longstanding friendship with the Jewish community.

As you well know, I believe that in our society we must be able to dialogue honestly and openly with one another, and that on both sides we must listen carefully to the honest expression of our friends—which is all the more reason why all of us engaged in public discourse must be especially sensitive to the realities of inter-group relations.

I look forward to further cooperation with you.

With all best wishes for a peaceful 1977.

Cordially,
Bertram H. Gold

Dear Bert:
Thank you very much for your recent, gracious letter. I'm glad that the regrettable misunderstandings can be brought to an end. As you remember, I was most reluctant to give the talk in the first place because I feared the reaction but agreed

to do so because I had been told that it could mark the opening of a new phase of Catholic-Jewish discussion. Like you, I felt that the reaction at the meeting, while mixed, was basically positive and friendly.

In retrospect, it would have been better if I had put more in the paper about what the Jewish community and AJC has already done to improve Catholic-Jewish relationships—though that was not my assignment. I also lament the fact that some of the language in the paper, hardly offensive in itself, could easily be misunderstood when excerpted out of context.

I, too, look forward to continued cooperation in the years ahead.

Shalom,
Andy

Andrew M. Greeley, a sociologist and Roman Catholic priest in the archdiocese of Chicago, is the author of over forty books, a syndicated newspaper columnist, the program director for the National Opinion Research Center at the University of Chicago, and presently the director of its Center for the Study of American Pluralism. *Time* magazine called Greeley "an informational machine gun who can fire off an article on Jesus to the *New York Times,* on ethnic groups to the *Antioch Review,* or on war to *Dissent.*"

Delaware